Is Anybody Up There?

Also by Paul Arnott

A Good Likeness

Let Me Eat Cake

Paul Arnott

Is Anybody Up There?

Adventures of a Devout Sceptic

SCEPTRE

First published in Great Britain in 2008 by Sceptre
An imprint of Hodder & Stoughton
An Hachette Livre UK company

1

Copyright © Paul Arnott 2008

The right of Paul Arnott to be identified as the Author
of the Work has been asserted by him in accordance
with the Copyright, Designs and Patents Act 1988.

All rights reserved. No part of this publication may be reproduced, stored
in a retrieval system, or transmitted, in any form or by any means without
the prior written permission of the publisher, nor be otherwise circulated in
any form of binding or cover other than that in which it is published and
without a similar condition being imposed on the subsequent purchaser.

A CIP catalogue record for this title is available from the British Library

ISBN 978 0 340 93679 5

Typeset in Sabon by Hewer Text UK Ltd, Edinburgh
Printed and bound by Clays Ltd, St Ives plc

Hodder & Stoughton policy is to use papers that are natural,
renewable and recyclable products and made from wood grown in
sustainable forests. The logging and manufacturing processes are expected
to conform to the environmental regulations of the country of origin.

Hodder & Stoughton Ltd
338 Euston Road
London NW1 3BH

www.hodder.co.uk

So my father said me, he said, what if it's all a joke, what if there isn't anybody up there? And I said to him, well, if it is a joke we'd better all make it a good one.

Kenneth Williams, 1974

But remember always, as I told you at first, that this is all a fairy tale, and only fun and pretence: and, therefore, you are not to believe a word of it, even if it is true.

Charles Kingsley, *The Water Babies*, 1863

Luton Cultural Services Trust	
9 39115090	
Askews	
2OH ARN	
2 0 FEB 2009	

Contents

Introduction

When I began to write this book, I didn't plan anything by way of introduction. Such chapters are often written when the author is still sharpening his pencil and dreaming of a Pulitzer prize. Freud wrote in the introduction to *The Interpretation of Dreams* that 'insight such as this falls to one's lot but once in a lifetime', unintentionally boasting of the work in hand while discounting anything he'd generate over the next thirty years. Like a field marshal, a writer is unwise to cede the element of surprise.

I especially didn't want to shout at the reader at the very beginning, because this book covers a lot of ground which will place it on the religious shelves as well as in sections on memoir and social history. It's a sensitive area. I'm fond of its title, which was someone else's idea, but am aware that it's shared by an American website run by a faith healer whose proudest claim is that she regenerated the shrivelled internal organs of an unborn child by praying with Mom. There's an easy way for a rational man to react to that, but the essence of my approach is to take a deep breath before doing so. A bombastic introduction in a book with a religious theme which hopes to quietly commend a laissez-faire approach when considering the different faiths fermenting and stirring across the planet could jeopardise its liberal mission.

However, circumstances have changed since I began writing, though not really in religious life itself. The recent fear of fundamentalism goes back centuries, and in our own times it can be dated to the overthrow of the Shah of Iran in 1979 and the resurgence of the theocratic state. Most have been aware of the difficulties with this for decades, but in this journalistic age the attack on the World Trade Center in 2001 has been identified, incorrectly, as its moment of genesis. I conceived this book years after all that, when themes of fundamentalism were already well discussed and had widened appropriately to look at a nutty minority of American Christians too. It was not religious fundamentalism which made an introduction to this book necessary; it was the rise of atheistic fundamentalism. What changed everything for me were the footsteps of a giant breaking into my quiet religious forest looking to uproot every single tree. These size eighteen boots belonged to Richard Dawkins, and the main purpose of writing this introduction is to make clear that my book was never designed as a reaction to him. It is its own thing.

I can identify its point of conception precisely. I was with my family on a holiday of a lifetime – six weeks in America billeted between family sofas and roadside motels. In week four of our transcontinental odyssey we were driving down the Big Sur Highway, which heads south from San Francisco and overlooks the Pacific for most of central California. It's an ordinary two-lane road in a deeply evocative place where there are seals and surfers dodging the odd great white shark in the freezing currents of the ocean. We were doing about fifty with the windows down when we passed a sight I hadn't seen in Britain for many years – a VW camper van spray-painted with peace signs and flowers, and the single word 'Perception' in a 'hey, man' scrawl across the front. One of the children asked why they'd done that to their car and I said, 'Because, children, we all have stupid thoughts, but hippies are people who write them on the front of their vans.'

With each passing mile after saying that, I felt worse. What a horrible, cynical thing to think, let alone say, in reply to an innocent question. I was my children's age when hippies first roamed the earth, on the whole as harmless and hopeful a bunch as mankind has ever produced. How had I, a lucky fellow on a wonderful trip, stooped to making a low quip at their expense? Immediately I thought of the man who'd been their epitome for a while, whose death in 1981 came as a different and individualistic mindset was on the rise. John Lennon, the last of the suburban gurus, might have been full of it, but he believed in something, even if it was only that 'in the end the love you take is equal to the love you make', as a Radio Caroline jingle used to tell us from a rusty boat every hour of the day.

So I pulled our people-mover over and we went for a walk in the Sequoia forest off the road, and as we walked I back-tracked fast. Actually, hippies were OK, I said, and the people who owned that car were probably really nice. There was nothing wrong in believing in things, I assured them. In the hot foothills of the Sierra Nevada, it felt very much the time and place to be straight about all this, as I began to think this could be my final testament. My imagination had been caught by a sign saying that in order to avoid crossing the path of a mountain lion we should keep talking loudly and possibly clap our hands as well. Deaths by mountain lion last year: 2.

We would have made an odd sight if there had been anyone else in the forest – a devoutly atheist wife and elder son walking with three other children, all clapping their hands, as a terrified-looking man with a sunburned pate answered a volley of questions about what he really believed in. As I marched on, I said that I'd have to begin at the beginning, and to my sincere surprise I realised that the very first entity I'd given credence to in my conscious life was fairies. I expected hoots of derision, but my adherents weren't so long themselves out of the tooth fairy, leprechauns and Father Christmas phase. There's complicity between adults and children when you talk about sweets, but I hadn't expected that belief, even formal religious belief, could be the same.

By the time we were back at the car, and entirely by accident, I had given them the outline of this book. By telling them about my own stumbling religious life, from Mr Singh the Sikh bus conductor to Anil the Hindu showing me his willy to prove he had one, from see-through robes at a Bromley baptism to Roger the Christian at the fish factory, it dawned on me that my entire life was set in a context which I had somehow ignored. Atheism was the default mindset for my generation, yet I was never more than a week away from a visit to an empty church, mosque, temple or synagogue. On holiday I always went to the religious spots of great cities first, even as my wife looked for the shops. I'd even ended up living in Church Street.

As we continued our mini epic voyage, I flipped open the laptop in a series of identical roadside motels and began to tap in my memories. America really sets the juices flowing on religious themes. We'd stayed with my wife's Irish Catholic family for a reunion in Iowa. They were a broad church, from closely related aunts and uncles who'd gone from living amongst the Inuit in Alaska to drilling for oil in Bible Belt Texas – good open-minded people – to the more distant relative standing in line for the barbecue next to me who celebrated the weekend wearing an 'Abortion Equals Murder' T-shirt.

In New York we'd eaten and sung at celebratory gospel breakfasts, but in LA we had seen black Pentecostalist churches struggling to save the lives and souls of boys in the 'hood. We'd followed the Mormon Trail across Nebraska, and seen the old Spanish Catholic missions dotted across California, and its ignored community of Mexican salad pickers in the San Fernando Valley of today. We'd stayed with a lovely friend of my wife's mother in Marin County, a fair-skinned widow, originally of Episcopalian roots in Connecticut, who was bound through her late husband to a wonderful Greek Orthodox congregation in San Francisco. And of course we'd hooted at the cable broadcasts by orange-faced evangelists and listened to them rant and rave on the radio as we'd crossed their continent.

That day of the hippy camper van and our walk in the lion-infested wood was filled with innocence and experience. Standing on the pier of an old whaling station at Pigeon Point, we saw a pod of migrating grey whales, an encounter of sacred mystery to the most sceptical. Later that afternoon we found a dark contrast with the essence of my Sequoia improvisation on religion at the huge house built by William Randolph Hearst perched on a hill above

San Simeon. Aping many architectural forms, most of them religious in origin, Hearst Castle was the epitome of the rich man's mansion. Big bucks had been spent to celebrate the media magnate himself – a Roman folly without an ounce of spirit or reverence or humility to be seen. This was not a godly house. It had been built by Mammon, and as we trooped round it with our guide, the Americans in our party knew it was not the best of their country and its aspirations, but the worst. Godlessness is nothing to boast about.

And so to Richard Dawkins. I didn't set out to tangle with him or his ilk. I'd always admired his ambition to attempt an explanation of human society through evolutionary biology, though since first studying *The Selfish Gene* as a psychology student twenty-five years ago, I knew that his extrapolations into altruism and faith were too deterministic, rich in some answers and impoverished in others. I was rather glum that *The God Delusion* had won such attention, not because of its ranting tone or because I found so much of it wrong, but because, in the words of Prince Myshkin in Dostoevsky's *The Idiot*, 'Atheists always seem to be talking about something else'.

To my mind, it was as if he'd written a book about football and only focused on the hooligans, corruption in the boardroom, and the few bent referees, ignoring the fantastic skills of both male and female players on the ball and the communal wonder which comes with the scoring of a goal. Dawkins railed against easy targets one after the other, without recognising that every religious person, other than the lunatic fringe he was tilting at, agreed with him wholly about life at the extremes of faith. When I think about religion, I'm not considering a simplistic answer to where the world came from, or whether a sky god is looking after me, if there is a tribal advantage to being in the same faith, or if I can find something to explain the supernatural, but disproving these aspects of religion seems to preoccupy Dawkins and the atheists. Of course they're not much use to anybody, but they are not what I'm talking about at all. My reflections come from the life I've led, the evidence of my own eyes.

Dawkins has been answered in the work of Alister McGrath, and, perhaps surprisingly, by a robust intellectual response from the Archbishop of Canterbury, Rowan Williams. The sincere, concerned and kind timbre of the work of Karen Armstrong is invaluable here, too, if one wants to see the religious picture in digital widescreen again after Dawkins's black and white. Beyond this point, he is not my main concern; though, with my knees slightly trembling, I must declare that his name will occasionally arise.

The main compensation for the unnatural pursuit of writing at a solitary desk is that it's a rare day when you're truly alone. My first book was about my being adopted, and when word of this escaped, all sorts of acquaintances called to declare their personal involvement in this secretive subject. When I then wrote about my lifelong love of sweet foods and the history of their making, others wanted to share their memories of favourite products and knocked at our door with tasty offerings. When I said I was going to write *Is Anybody Up There?* there was another universal reaction. If I'd had a pound for everyone who cracked a joke about fatwas, I'd have had enough for a bullet-proof vest. I replied to the jokers that since they didn't know a fatwa was not actually a death sentence but a mullah's proclamation of Koranic authority on anything from shrine repairs to what to eat for breakfast, it was just as well someone was writing this book. Though if they did not care to read it, I advised, it would not be necessary for them to visit a mosque – they could obtain guidance at *muftisays.com*, *efatwa.com* and even *askimam.com*. The more interesting, secondary response reminded me of the adoption story. I was astonished by how many agnostics wanted to share their hidden family backgrounds, in the Plymouth Brethren, the Quakers, assimilated Judaism. Experiences of brushes with the Moonies or Hare Krishna seemed pedestrian compared to these repressed tales of families leaving their religion behind them. Gone but seemingly never forgotten.

Finally, I was often asked, how on earth are you going to do this? And, *Is* there Anybody up there? Well, I said, to answer the first question first (and I wouldn't want to make Freud's mistake here), I do wonder if in this loquacious modern world a religious anecdote told today might not be the contemporary equivalent of a parable. And to answer the even trickier one, I said they'd really have to read the book to find out.

Silver Spoons

I made my religious debut before an adoring audience on a wet and chilly April afternoon. Inside, it was candlelit, abundant with fresh flowers, but outside I was sheltered from the sleet by well-wishers holding umbrellas. My garment for the occasion had been decided long before, and despite the rain we went ahead with it: a full-length ivory frock, featuring puffed sleeves and a dainty little bow on my chest. Beneath the frock, my legs were bare except for short white socks and soft leather shoes with silver buckles. My sparse hair, then blonde, was kissed into a curl at the front.

The man supervising my coming-out was also wearing a frock, embroidered in gold patterns cascading to the hemline of his lengthy train, which was as white as his hair. When he moved, his train was held away from the cold floor in the fingers of a young man. He wore white too, his own little number exposing the bulge of an adolescent Adam's apple.

I only know all this from photographs of the ceremony, a celebration of my uniqueness the like of which has not happened since. I have no memory of the ritual myself. Apparently I spent much of it weeping before falling asleep in the arms of my mother, Betty. In the sideboard of the family home where she still lives, there is a small horde of silver offerings brought by guests to honour the occasion. Teaspoons, egg cups, and a napkin ring engraved with my initials, P.A.A. For the next fourteen years another memento lay unopened in a silver cardboard box, also bearing a tiny bow: a sliver of commemorative christening cake.

We opened the box on the day I was confirmed and found that, while the sugars had perfectly preserved it, the cardboard had developed a moist fungus fed by the marzipan. That was a very different afternoon to my christening – I was a hairy youth making an uncertain commitment to follow a saviour just a few days after I'd been caned at school. Plus I was wearing trousers.

That all came much later. My christening was an unremembered prelude to an early childhood of typically unfettered fantasies about the nature of the strange world into which I was born. Though I was baptised at St George's Bickley, south London outpost of the Dickensian Diocese of Rochester, for the next five years, before my father brought me back, I was a lifeform all Christians fear. I was, unknowingly and with the best will in the world, a pure little pagan.

Mrs Do-As-You-Would-Be-Done-By

In the innocent days before I'd have worried about its contents, I gave my mother the envelope from school and ran through the back door to the bottom of the garden. Lying on my front on the damp grass, I leaned forward over the pond next to the rockery where the pungent waterweeds glistened in the afternoon sun.

It was important to stay silent. The only sound was the sudden slurps of fantailed goldfish sucking midges into the water through pink lips. Indoors, my mother, Betty, finished the letter and put it on the mantelpiece for my father to see when he got home from work.

'Paul,' she called through the back door.

'Shush,' I whispered.

The landscape under my nose was ruled over by a colony of easily disturbed little people with wings. They had wings so that they could fly away from dangerous fish lips or garden-spider fangs. I could fly too, but only when I was asleep. I realised that when I was awake, my size, relative to the garden fairies, didn't allow for wings. This would be different if and when I became an angel, but I'd be dead then, or at least have heaven as my principal domicile. Fairies had struck a different deal. They could have wings now, but it would make them titchy to the point of invisibility.

'I've just read the letter, dear,' said my mother as she came down the garden path. 'It's from Mr Schofield.'

I was five. I hadn't considered that my headmaster had a name. Just 'Sir'.

'Yes, a very nice surprise.'

I launched some acorn shells for the fairies to sail in when they emerged from their crevice dwellings after I'd gone.

'You've won a prize, dear.'

'Who from?'

'The school. They say it's for "four-year-old progress".'

'I'm not four.'

'Yes, dear. But they give it for the last year, you see.'

She'd lost me. And the fairies would never come out now.

'What's the prize?'

'It's a lovely book.'

I'd have preferred sweets.

'What book?'

'The teachers think you might like to read *The Water Babies*.

'I don't like baby books.'

'It's not about babies. They're more like fairies, really. Ones that live under the water.'

I wanted a glass of milk now, so I brushed the mud off my knees and dashed inside, hopeful of a jam ring too.

'Can I see the book, please?'

'Soon. Not quite yet. They're presenting it to you next weekend. In the Town Hall.'

I clambered on to a high stool by the breakfast bar and caught the extra-bouncy rubber ball as it flew back from the floor towards me. Putting the broken telescope my grandad had given me to my eye, I scanned the garden for fairies.

My mother seemed unable to get on with her housework.

'Yes, the Mayor of Bromley will be there. Well, you'll be all right for a minute, won't you, dear? I think I'll just pop next door and tell Jean.'

I sat alone, supping milk and making crumbs. I could not have known, as I watched out for a flight of fairies, that by the end of that summer they would be the first otherworldly entities I wholly believed in which I was able to prove were not real.

What had led this little boy, in the year when they were putting flowers in their hair in San Francisco, to believe there were fairies at the bottom of the garden? The explanation is surprisingly rational if now widely overlooked.

The age of Queen Victoria had been at its zenith a full hundred years before. With two world wars and a nascent social revolution since, its shadow should have passed, but in fact it was everywhere. Many of my friends lived in red-brick Victorian houses with spooky turrets and tiled hallways, even if the fireplaces were boarded over for North Sea gas. We played at the top of suburban staircases as Victorian children had, still eavesdropped through the spindles on the adults below as they prepared to go out.

A century earlier the adults might have demanded that the children come downstairs and taken them to a new art gallery funded by a philanthropist like William Hesketh Lever, who sold his Sunlight soap by a new method also bequeathed to us from then – mass-market advertising. In the gallery we would not have been detained by the old masters, but would have headed for the exciting new work by Landseer, Millais, and Turner which depicted fluttering fairies in their realm in a haze of innocence or debauchery or even borderline bestiality.

Later on in the evening, the family might have seen startling sights at the theatre, especially in *The Tempest* or *A Midsummer Night's Dream*, where the sensation of seeing fairies fly and dance was as beguiling as a new effects movie today. The sets were inspired by the galleried art, which itself became even more inspired by the frenzy of movement and aerial accomplishment worked by ace teams of wire-men backstage. Some of these artists were quite mad – the murderer Richard Dadd, for one, who killed his father and spent the rest of his life in Bedlam producing intricate and unparalleled depictions of fairyland. He may have been the only murderer living in the fairy realm, but others had their minds bent too by the opiates they took for aches and pains, their visions further inflamed by imbibing cocaine.

This rash of fairy art had spread following the sudden rise in 1840s New York of the séance, an epidemic of speaking to the dead which soon crossed the Atlantic and inveigled otherwise sensible men such as Sir Arthur Conan Doyle. The British Psychic Society expressed the will of these spiritualists from its HQ in Belgrave Square, and its pseudo-scientific practices gave credence to the idea that there were definitely worlds beyond the known and seen. If there was a land of the dead, then why not a fairyland too?

Victorian Britain would have been fertile ground for all this. Many lives were insecure. With industrialisation, displacement was rife. There was a yearning for an uncorrupted, pre-industrial innocence, and many of the new city-dwellers were not long arrived from parts of Western England, Ireland and Wales where a fairy mythology of pixies and hobgoblins still thrived – the realm of Robin Goodfellow made Puckish by Shakespeare's *Midsummer Night's Dream*. John Anster Fitzgerald, aka 'Fairy' Fitzgerald, played on this brilliantly, infusing his art with the Celtic myths of his Irish homeland, an inspiration to many others.

So, even as the British Empire took hold of wealth and land on a scale never seen before, at home its people were indulging in the art and theatre of an unseen underworld. Yet they were still short of first-rate written material to feed this hunger. The seeds for its provision had been sown in France a hundred years before, when Charles Perrault, a civil servant who had overseen the construction of Versailles, collated the traditional oral stories of *Little Red Riding Hood*, *Cinderella* and *Sleeping Beauty* for the first time. Britain wasn't at ease with French produce then, but it was prepared to accept the works of the German 'Brothers' Grimm, Wilhelm and Jacob, who followed the example of Perrault and recorded well-known folk tales such as *Snow White* and *Rumpelstiltskin*. These were a publishing phenomenon and incited even more frenetic fairy-painting activity, developing alongside Pre-Raphaelite art. Both literature and art reflected the Germanic respect for folklore and ancient cults widely admired by British intellectuals.

How on earth did all this get to me? Fairies were meant to have been done for twice over. First, they'd been destroyed by the invention of photography. Where once a painter could stare into a rockery or the grotto of a great estate and see in his mind's eye a train of fairy carriages and elves, his usurper the photographer could prove that there was nothing there at all. Famous attempts were made to forge fairy photographs, but these hoaxes only hastened their demise. The optimistic Edwardians at the dawn of the twentieth century seemed to have a diminished desire to imagine little winged people fluttering across their sleeping faces, and when their over-confidence imploded into war in 1914, sprites and fairies were evicted from the adult imagination for ever.

Not so, however, in the psyches of children. Fairy dust had been blasted high into the atmosphere and it fell on those of us with any kind of capacity for fantasy. Besides, as a boy, my world was so full of oddities that I'd have believed almost anything. My storybooks, enjoyed by children two generations earlier, fuelled my imagination – *Peter Pan*, illustrated by Arthur Rackham (who'd also brought Shakespeare's Titania and Bottom to life years before), *Tom Thumb* and the illustrated and abbreviated *Arabian Nights*, full of djinns and spirits.

Moreover, my daily five-year-old life seemed to be populated with essentially benign relations and friends of my parents who might have been drawn by George Cruickshank, who gave Britain such evocative pictures for the tales of the Brothers Grimm that he was asked to do the German editions too. His books were still in our local children's library on Crown Lane, and in his engravings I spotted characters I might bump into any week in Bromley, including old ladies with warts, hunchbacks, dwarves and a giant who was Britain's tallest man. Even the hippy visages of young men and women growing wild hair for a summer or two re-minded me of the creatures stalking Grimm German forests. That *The Elves and the Shoemaker* was more documentary than fiction seemed to me beyond doubt.

There wasn't any fairy art on the walls of Bromley Town Hall, though lots of aldermen in chains of office looked down at us from well-varnished frames as we gathered to go into the presentation. My dad could look splendid when he wanted to – a bit of a tan, grey suit, white shirt, light grey tie. My mum stood next to him in her fur. Happily she was not wearing the wig she'd bought at the hair equivalent of a Tupperware party. Women of middle years had odd-coloured hair in those days – pink and blue and even purple – but this wig was somewhere between brown and green. It lived on a block in a box in her wardrobe, which was where it belonged.

The prize recipients were led into an antechamber and instructed in how we should conduct ourselves when being presented with our books. Indeed, we were shown what to do, and forced to practise it. I was outraged. This was the first occasion when I learnt there really is no such thing as a free lunch.

We filed into the hall and the ceremony began. I didn't hear a word. All I wanted was this book, but the thing I was going to have to do to get it went against my entire nature.

When my name was called I did precisely as I'd been told. I walked to a door at the side of the stage, went up a short flight of stairs out of view, and marched across from the wings to the waiting Lady Mayoress. She was holding out my book, which looked pretty inviting, but before I could accept it I had orders to follow. I had to curtsy. I was furious – the fastest boy in the playground reduced to bending his knee like a great big pansy. Apparently my face was thunderous as I came down the stairs on the other side of the stage. I took my original seat and deliberately didn't watch or listen to another word of the occasion. I opened the book instead.

'*The Water Babies*,' it said. 'Retold from the story by Charles Kingsley.' A decorated label was gummed on the facing page inside: 'Prize Awarded to Paul Arnott (Kindergarten) for 4-year-old progress', signed by 'J. Schofield, Headmaster, May 1967'.

In 1863 the Reverend Kingsley wrote the story of Tom, a boy who fell into a stream, where he didn't drown but grew gills and lived amongst the water nymphs and fairies.

It expressed much of the lifelong grief he suffered over the drowning of his brother, Herbert, many years before. Children are receptive to the potency of such true inspiration, even when the author's imagination carries him to the Arctic, where whales die peacefully in a safe and sheltered pool cared for by a good old lady away from the harpoons of cruel whalers. That passage directly inspired a lifelong fascination in whales. My dad had to ask me to stop reading it as I walked around at the finger buffet after the prize-giving with my nose in the pages. I only stopped to watch the mayoral party leave in a black Daimler with huge windows and the town crest flying from a flag on the bonnet.

When we got home, I lay on my bed with my arms straight above my head and read on until I had finished. My dad was listening to the football results on the radio when I came out, and my mum was making my favourite beans on toast for supper. Saturday was the only day in the week when she didn't cook a full meal.

Outside in the garden I looked into the rockery pond. Things were more complex under the water than I had imagined. Tom had fallen into a place like this and been carried to the sea to meet Mrs Do-As-You-Would-Be-Done-By and Mrs Be-Done-By-As-You-Did. He was changed from a dirty little sweep, suddenly ashamed when he saw his filthy skin in the bedroom mirror of a great house where a beautiful girl slept, via all the waters in the world, into a morally complete young man who fell in love with the girl when they were much older.

A poor swimmer at that age, I knew I wouldn't last a moment if I fell into a stream. I didn't expect to grow gills, to talk to a whale by an iceberg, or meet Mother Carey at the Other-end-of-No-where, yet I read this book over and over again and lived in its illustrations. I kept it safely by my bed, never taking it outside to the garden to share with the invisible folk who lived in the rockery. They were mute and did not read. *The Water Babies* was the inspired work of a classic Victorian clergyman whose acceptance of Darwin's theory of evolution left him filled with doubt but with an abundant interest in natural history.

I took *The Water Babies* on holiday to Cornwall that summer, where we stayed in a hotel overlooking Praa Sands. This holiday was notable as the first occasion when I drank Coca-Cola with dinner, and for the evening walk afterwards with my parents when I did not have to imagine seeing fairies in the bushes; I actually saw them.

Of course I saw them. I'd spent enough from my mother's purse in wishing wells from St Ives to Land's End to make it true. This was plainly the county of the hobgoblin and the elf; its tourist spots sold souvenirs celebrating the many manifestations of the Cornish pixie. If I'd been a girl I'd have loved to own one of the pixie charms designed to hang from a bracelet next to a tiddly horseshoe or a thatched cottage.

Yet somehow my parents hadn't noticed these night-time fairies as we sauntered past them along the coastal path with the waves crashing below. I was surprised myself by their sheer luminescence. Like Tinker Bell, their features were hidden in a ball of light, which flashed as they jumped from twig to twig. My parents were a few steps ahead and I couldn't fathom why they hadn't stopped to witness this extraordinary scene – hundreds of white fairies sparkling in the darkness.

Finally, I asked them to stop and look. My dad saw how captivated I was as I pointed into the bush.

'Fairies,' I said.

'Ah, yes,' he said. 'We don't seem to get these in London these days, do we? I used to love them when I was a boy.'

He peered closer and his eyes were lit as if by a weak torch.

'Lovely, aren't they? Of course, they might not actually be fairies as such. These are more like glow worms. A bit like fairies, though, I'll grant you. Look at this, everyone, Paul's found some glow worms.'

I accepted credit for this with repressed embarrassment, relieved that I hadn't made more of my being the first human ever to discover a fairy colony on a Cornish path near the cliff edge. Before bedtime, back at the hotel, I hung about in the games room watching older children play table tennis, trying to forget. They had a new LP on the turntable with a jolly song called 'When I'm Sixty Four'. I was glad of its jaunty lilt, because somewhere inside I was grieving the realisation that fairies didn't exist outside my head. It was a cold feeling. This probably meant the tooth fairy wasn't real either.

Then another song began to fill the large open attic, and to my young ears it sounded like hell, madness, such an uneasy din that I decided to leave the games room rather than hear it out. For while I'd been talking to imps in Bromley, George Harrison had been learning to meditate with the Maharishi Mahesh Yogi in Rishikesh, India, and from an astral plane decided to impose five minutes of screeching sitar on 'Sergeant Pepper's Lonely Hearts Club Band'.

I went back to my room and realised that behind the plywood there was a massive chimney feeding up from the ground floor and through my room, coming out to the stack I could see on the roof as I looked up at the hotel from the beach. And I remembered the end of *The Water Babies*, when Tom's mercy for the horrible Grimes moved the nasty old sweep to weep tears, which dissolved the mortar of a chimney in which he seemed to have been wedged for eternity. And I knew that even if fairies didn't exist, there had to be some good reason why we willed them into being.

By George

The morning after my disenchantment by glow worm, we were going home. Motorway service stations weren't widespread then, and in any case Betty hated the Little Chef, from his fat white face to his pointy toes. Our holiday climaxed after breakfast on the final morning by the kitchen door of the hotel, where a kind proprietor was packing us some lunch for the road. The Cornish kept their pasties in-county in those days, so our cardboard box was loaded with egg sandwiches, apples, salted crisps and slices of pork pie.

There was a ritual about the journey home from the West. My parents owned a book published by the AA called *Treasures of Britain*. They always brought it with them, and my father, Peter, always browsed through it on the bonnet for any attractions en route. Then we'd set off for London and stop for lunch at Stonehenge anyway. This monument at a high point on Salisbury Plain was known to us south Londoners for two reasons. One, it was halfway home. Two, nobody knew what it was there for.

As the years rolled by we heard tell of Celts and Druids, ley lines and archaeoastronomers. We saw television programmes recreating the rolling of vast stones. We hooted at the useless replica used in the film of *Tess*, made in Normandy because of the arrest warrant for Roman Polanski. Above all we howled at the fourteen-inch version danced around by dwarves in the mockumentary film *This Is Spinal Tap* during their cod-concept song 'Stone 'enge', which Nigel Tufnell had intended would stand at a priapic fourteen feet.

Back then, in the schools of England, the Celts and Druids were ignored. Occasionally you'd see a muddy Druid on the news ripping his clothes off at the summer solstice. But there was no exegesis, relying on sorts of myths, archaeological punditry and à la carte pickings from Irish sagas. It looked like fun, and nobody was ever lost to the Druids as they were to cults like the Moonies. Perceived as harmless, so long as any witchery was white, they had a reputation as a refuge for young idlers. As for we capitalist holidaymakers returning to the smoke, our history only began in 1066. We weren't at all sure who the Ancient Britons were, except that they were led by a man who couldn't master cake-baking.

So, what could have been a natural progression in my spiritual journey from a lost faith in the netherworlds of fairies and demons and little people to a rubric of green men and wizards and warlocks never took hold. This supposedly evocative location just didn't evoke. The honest motorist of southern England with his egg sandwich was bored by Stonehenge. It was a monolith he couldn't integrate into his national identity because it was built in 2,700 BC, when his ancestors could have been described as anything but English. England hadn't been invented. Nobody could tell you why it was constructed or what it was properly called. The Romans referred to it as *Circea Gigantum* (Giant's Ring). The Anglo-Saxons referred to it as *Stan-heng*. Betty used to make a fine chocolate dessert called *Charlotte Katrine* with an outer wall of erect sponge fingers, and we called that Stonehenge too, when she wasn't listening.

As far as my father's generation was concerned it was a car park with no historical or religious resonance whatsoever, and anyone making Druidical or other claims was spouting nonsense. Indeed, as he bowled about aimlessly between the standing stones he must have decided that, as I'd begun to see fairies hopping in the hedgerows on my mother's watch, it was time for him to step in. Steering the car in the direction of Andover and points east, he declared that next weekend he and I would become reacquainted with St George's church in Bickley.

Later that evening, having negotiated the Hog's Back and a pre-

M25 orbit of Outer London, Betty unpacked our suitcases and Peter sat at a table with an inevitably complicated motor insurance claim, the analysis and settling of which was the work he would return to in the morning. I fetched my Action Man from my bedroom downstairs and took him out into the garden to explore. I'd been careful before where I'd put him in the area near the small pond, not wanting to scare the little people, but now they were not there I placed him on the ledge with water running down it, where they used to fish, and watched him fight his way up the fjord to explode a Heavy Water plant. He became my familiar now, a mini-me adventurer who accompanied me everywhere. With a cold look in his eye and a livid scar he was a 'shoot now, think later' kind of guy. If the fairies ever did come back, he'd know how to deal with them.

Understanding now how Peter was often frustrated by his work, I realise that taking me back to the place of my christening the next weekend would not have been his idea of the perfect Sunday morning. Our attending St George's was not even logical. It involved a two-mile drive, when we lived next door to one church and two hundred yards from another. If it had been Betty making the choice, it would have made sense. St George's was set in an affluent part of the borough of Bromley where the five-acre gardens of Bickley villas built a hundred years earlier were being landscaped into exclusive estates, the original houses turned into residential homes or simply demolished. My mother approved of St George's on the grounds of social aspiration. St Luke's just down the road from our front door was a working church, where what one wore to Evensong was of little consequence. In the aisles of St George's, however, the swoosh of fur made a social mark. In reality, this nice distinction was academic because Betty would not be coming with us. Like millions of others, she had her own sincerely held creed: 'You don't have to go to church to be a Christian.'

My father didn't believe that at all. He had a wad of nineteenth-century sermons preached by one of his grandfathers stashed in his desk next to his accounts book. He was very light on detail on where this forefather had preached, but it was clear from their impenetrable tone that it was no evangelical or dissenting chapel. It must have been High Church.

St George's was very High Church indeed. We parked in the private road with potholes, entered through the gate, and crossed the graveyard to the door, an encounter with the dead I never became used to. Once inside, we were coshed by the heaving organ, and our breathing was made tighter by the incense wafting like morning mist amongst the pews.

I went to sit down, but my father hauled me up by my collar and, to my fury, made me do one of those curtsy things again in the direction of the altar. For his own part, he went down on one knee, flicking his hands across his chest in a cross pattern, and with some effort stood up and slid in beside me.

On the impractical narrow ledge fixed to the pew in front was a day's worth of paperwork. On the huge pillars soaring up to the ceiling was a board with random numbers for something called Psalms and something I had heard of called Hymns. I tried to work out how all this bureaucratic stuff interrelated, dropped some of it on the floor, hit my head on the ledge on the way back up and got ready for the show.

Suddenly everyone stood up. So did I, a sapling in a Redwood forest, unable to see beyond ranks of overcoats. The organ was pounding like thunder again, and after a minute I felt the air being displaced along my row by an approaching mass. I looked left and glimpsed a long procession of what might, I reasoned, be angels dressed in white robes passing up the aisle. I couldn't see the faces, but their numbers were impressive. There was a gap of a few seconds, and then I saw the big angel in the robe from my christening photograph, the one displayed by Betty on our mantelpiece downstairs, as he floated through. I was glad about this. The welfare of angels was beginning to worry me. How did they share British airspace with the new Phantom fighter jet of which we were so proud? Surely angels were quicker in the air than the *Flying*

Nun on television, but could they outrun a jet? Were there sometimes collisions? Never mind, I was entranced.

A host of cassocked minors billowed incense around him as he glided towards the altar, which looked like an outsize lime lozenge topped with white and gold paraphernalia. He swept towards it, and the minor attendants dropped away as the older men in plain black and white outfits took his staff and held open a sacred text. Then it began, a moaning as indecipherable to me as the issuances of a humpback whale. He must have been using structured language, but by the time it reached my ears it had broken down into a monotone whine with the odd pause for breath.

Then he looked up, with his very old-man white hair and watery blue eyes, smiled meekly, and the next thing I knew we were singing 'All Things Bright and Beautiful'. Peter looked down at me as I joined in – we'd practised this one at school – but no sooner had I begun to enjoy it than I began to feel annoyed. Halfway up the chancel stood opposing rows of choristers not satisfied with the ordinary melody which sufficed for the rest of us. Their thrills came from soaring harmonies and counterpoint and all manner of showing off, particularly in the last verse. I didn't see why, for not keeping to the tune, they should not be sacked.

Thus a rhythm was established. A bout of moaning from the feeble bellows of Father Glaser, a tuneful hymn partially ruined by the choir, a session on my knees fidding with the braiding on my hassock, and then a purposeful but incomprehensible movement of cassocked personnel to various parts of the church. Then the rhythm was broken by a red-faced man in Sunday best thrusting the midnight-blue collection purse with wooden handles at me to be passed along the row. It wasn't a promising start. All that kept me going was that my father's middle name was the same as the church. Little things like that matter to a child.

As we drove home from our first Bickley service, we passed the football pitches at the local rec where the teams were smoking at half-time. My spirits rose for a few seconds when I realised that my dad was parking the Austin Cambridge just outside the newsagents on Chatterton Road. This meant sweets, and frankly I'd earned them. Actually, it didn't. Peter went to the other side of the shop, where the rubber bands and invoice books were sold, and bought a slim red notebook. I was pretty disappointed when we left with this as his only purchase, but this was mitigated when he pulled out half a dozen stickers he'd collected at the back of the church from his jacket pocket and invited me to fix them on to the lined pages of the memo book.

Poor adults. How is it that they never know enough about the latest developments in a materialistic world: I loved stickers – of soldiers, tanks, cartoon characters, slogans. I had a sub-set of ones relating to motor sport – Michelin, Goodyear, Duckhams Motor Oil – but the stickers Peter pressed into my hand had me looking out of the car window to check that nobody had seen. There was an angel, a St Peter, a Jesus, a Moses, a Lamb of God and a view of Jerusalem, none of which could ever compete with the slick new range featuring the Batmobile.

At home on the dining room table before Sunday lunch I dutifully stuck Moses in at the front, but as Betty watched me through the serving hatch and Peter hovered, sipping his half-pint of beer, they already knew that in the battle for my soul involving Sunday church and holy stickers, the cause was lost. Moreover, it was not at all clear what either of them really believed themselves, and this uncertainty communicated itself to me.

Peter and I carried on like this for a while longer. I think the reason we stopped going was that even though he plainly had belief of a sort, he couldn't bear inflicting the crushing boredom on me. More importantly, he couldn't stand inflicting it on himself. It's not as if the two of us were not good at supporting lost causes. We spent every other Saturday afternoon watching Charlton Athletic for fifteen years. At least Charlton got us out into the open air. At least they seemed to be trying. At St George's, both a five-year-old child and a forty-five-year-old man were as alienated by the rituals of our nation's worship – the Church of England – as millions of others. Perhaps a man has to leave in order to find his way back, but it seems unfortunate that I'd learned how epically boring church can be before I'd realised it wasn't just a ceremony like the Changing of the Guard but something I was meant to be taking as the gospel truth.

Not that we'd abandoned St George's entirely. We went at Christmas, like the average Briton. After we'd paid homage to the tree, the turkey, the presents, the decorations, the pudding, the guests and the Queen, there was no reason not to give the church a moment's thought too. It was all a bit of a kerfuffle. The hymns weren't called hymns any more, they were carols. There were some new words to learn: crib, manger, frankincense, Herod. There was a big surprise in store as well.

To me, as to most children my age, this was a celebration of two great people. First of all, of course, there was the man the whole thing was named after, Father Christmas. Then there was a baby called Jesus, who seemed to have been born around the same time. After the children's candlelit service that year we visited the nativity scene at the back of St George's, and Peter explained that the doll in the straw had a second name. Christ. Jesus Christ. After whom Christ-mas was named. I asked what 'mas' meant but he declined to answer. I wondered how Father Christmas felt about this, and Peter elaborated on his point. Christmas was when Jesus was born and Easter was when we celebrated him dying. He pointed to a crucifix on the other side of the church. Easter was good, he said, because though he died on the cross he came back to life again.

I'd had enough. What a load of rot. This was the first I'd heard of it, and I was not alone, for in the Bible lessons we were being taught at school, this failed character didn't come into it. We were too busy learning how the world began.

In the Beginning . . .

As a child I used to have a lot of dreams where I was enormous in a landscape of midgets or tiny in a land of giants. Developmental psychologists from Freud to Piaget suggest there is a particular age when a child must stop believing he is the centre of the world and realise that the external environment is not always benign. It makes small philosophers of us all.

At six we're not really ready to process where we came from in biological terms, but there is a big question which we do like to discuss, remote enough to be safe. When did the world begin? Across the planet there are a hundred explanations, but in Miss Edan's form at South Bromley College there was only one. It was on her desk set high on a dais in the full-length bay window of our classroom overlooking the traffic on Masons Hill. It was a Bible, and it was older even than Miss Edan.

Only one book in the Bible mattered to Miss Edan, and that was Genesis. Not later parts about incest or concubines or Sodom and Gomorrah. Miss Edan concentrated on the beginning, twenty chapters spread over fifteen pages which are the most compressed work of narrative in our civilisation. She was cunning, too. Her lessons were not fire or brimstone, and oranges were not her only fruit. She read us *Dr Dolittle, Peter Pan* and *Thomas the Tank Engine*, and just when our guard was down she'd open that big black book on her desk and feed us another slice of the creation myth which has been central to our culture for thousands of years.

That the account she was introducing us to was true was a given. Miss Edan only dealt in the truth. The facts of the creation of the planet on which I stood were amply explained by her from the first ten chapters of Genesis. First, there'd been a void and a nothingness, which was like my dreams, so I bought that. Then God wanted to do something with this empty space so he created the world and all life upon it, taking six busy days and resting on the seventh. So far so good. Page one of the Bible and I was happy to endorse the lot.

Then the themes became more adult. In the Garden of Eden, Eve was tempted by a serpent to eat an apple from the Tree of Knowledge and persuaded her nervous partner Adam to do the same. God had warned them not to do this and so as a punishment he condemned men to lives of toil and women to painful labour, a hankering for men, and second place in the pecking order. Having delivered his sentence, God then expelled both Adam and Eve from Eden.

To us six-year-old children in the late sixties this was a bit heavy, man. It sort of explained why we all wore clothes, but it seemed tough on Adam and Eve, especially Eve. Miss Edan was a bluestocking spinster, so she didn't dwell much on her sexes inferior lot. She didn't dally long with Adam and Eve's disappointing offspring either, their first-born Cain slaying brother Abel and doomed to wander the land east of Eden with a special mark on his forehead. Fortunately Cain found a wife on his travels and begat Enoch, who begat Irad, who begat Mehujael and so on, until his descendants discovered music and how to make tools from bronze and iron. Mankind seemed to be finally out of the woods.

What most impressed us was that in these early days God allowed this dysfunctional family to live to a very great age. Had Miss Edan really just read out that Methuselah finally shuffled off at 969, having begat plenty including a diligent grandson called Noah, the first action hero? Miss Edan could hardly fail with this one. Which primary school teacher can resist Noah's Ark, a perfectly rounded story of wickedness becoming new hope? It seemed both men and women were full of this wickedness, and the men had particular difficulty in dealing with female beauty, so God put them on special measures. One, there'd be no more giants, though there hadn't been any mention of them before. Two, the best you could hope for now was to die aged 120. Three, unless you were friend or family of Noah, a mature 600 at the time, or one of a pair of any animal on Earth, you were to be obliterated by a global flood. Just to make sure you didn't tread water, this flood would last forty days and the only viable craft would be a homemade ship skippered by Noah, a triple-decker, 133 metres long, 22 metres wide and 13 metres high (300 × 50 × 30 in cubits). The British engineering glory of my childhood was the *QEII* ocean liner. Noah's Ark was about half its size.

At last, a bit of adventure in the Bible. When the flood receded Noah made a few sacrifices and then God made something which appeared absolutely brilliant to a six-year-old. He was so sincerely apologetic about the flooding that to reassure mankind he would never do it again he gave them a mark in the sky to remind them of his promise. He invented the rainbow, and pledged to send millions more rainbows as fresh reminders of his covenant. That was show business and it made good sense to me.

Miss Edan pinned up a poster of Noah's ark on the back of the classroom door, showing pairs of ducks and elephants disembarking on to shore as the waters vanished down a muddy plughole. Noah and his wife beamed happily from the bridge, and in the sky that first rainbow issued from the hand of an otherwise unseen God. There was even a song for all this – 'The Animals Went in Two By Two, Hurrah, Hurrah' – which I would hum as I chucked my lion about in the bath. Action Man used to shepherd my own menagerie into an ark which had started as an Airfix battleship, but after decommissioning made a safe vessel for a shark and four piglets, with room for a police car and a small supply of Action Man's German-style hand grenades, just in case.

So an elderly lady with an Edwardian upbringing had successfully introduced her class to the wonders of the Bible. It became a harder sell from there on. In the middle sections of Genesis, what passed for a universal account of the beginning of the world became a sorry tale of people called Hebrews. Either they were going about their daily business convinced they were God's chosen people with right of tenure in a land called Canaan, or they were pissing him off so mightily that he made them sterile, diseased or enslaved to the Egyptians for what seemed to us (and was) centuries.

The theological idea she could not lead us through was the one story we had to buy. We couldn't imagine a time when there was more than one God. What would you need any more for? Yet she had to convince us that a man called Abraham was the first to make a covenant with someone called Yahweh that he would be the only God of the Hebrews.

Miss Edan told us this in grave terms from her high chair behind the desk, but we couldn't quite grasp the significance. Indeed, disaster struck most of us when she attempted to tell us how God became convinced that the man who would be regarded as the founding father of Judaism, Christianity and Islam, and the many flavours of all three, was to be completely trusted.

Apparently Abraham had taken his only son, Isaac (the illegitimate first son, Ishmael, begat from a roll in the hay with his wife's maid Hagar didn't count) for a long walk up a mountain. There, he tied Isaac up, sharpened a knife, laid some kindling and prepared to stab and roast him for the approval of God.

It was madness. We could all see that. Miss Edan's eyes glowed as she tried to explain the wonder of this. Many of her generation were very familiar with the idea of sacrifice, financial, emotional, material. The pain of it brought them closer to purity of spirit. But to be prepared to kill your own son? This was tough love, and made some of us wonder if our own fathers might throw us on the garden bonfire one day in exchange for divinity.

She was beginning to lose her flock. But not me. I don't know what was wrong with me – I was a credulous idiot, perhaps. My friends had sealed over their ears before the main act had even been introduced. It was His omission from what we were being taught which was the oddest thing of all. Where was the Christ in Christianity? He was already well down in the polls compared with Father Christmas, and there were even doubts about him. Whether at St George's or at school, Jesus hardly got a mention. What we learned about was his dad and all his workings. The suspicion was that Jesus might be a pretty disappointing kind of hero, a chump who, even as the son of God, managed to get himself killed. He was like the inheritor of a great estate, not guilty of gambling or wenching the big house away but, worse, actually giving it away. Who'd do that?

It might have been better for all of us children, inoculated so early against matters of religion, if we'd been allowed to know it was not all meant to be true. We'd been enjoying a creation myth, one of the very best, but Miss Edan would have possessed the knowledge to take us into all sorts of other worlds and their versions of the great beginning. She might have worried that this would risk our interest in the tale from her favourite book, but children love the opportunity to explore by making comparisons.

Today a teacher of her quality would speak freely of the great god Ra in Egypt rising from the universal sea called Nu and making the first day, how his burning tears dropped on to the banks of the Nile and made the first man and woman. We'd already drawn Vikings and their longboats for her, but how much more interesting they'd have seemed if we'd known that Odin, King of the Gods, made a woman by breathing on driftwood on a beach, then a man the same way. How he gave them the power of speech and called them Elm and Ash.

She would have known, too, about the very first civilisation in recorded history, the Sumerians, from the land later carved out as Iraq, with their story of the sun god, Marduk, tearing Tiamat the salty sea in two and thus making the arc of the sky and the world of men. And what was significant about this was that the Sumerians knew this wasn't true. They understood that of course creation was unfathomable, but they engaged with it by making stories none the less.

Miss Edan didn't tell us this. She did her best, but by accident presented us with a binary choice: believe it or not. We knew there must be more to it than that.

My eyes were opened to a world elsewhere on a London bus.

Knights of the Road

The very last London Routemaster bus was decommissioned early in the new millennium, which pained many Londoners, who'd simply loved them. It makes me feel ancient to recall that they only entered into use when I was a child, their endearing snouts and ocular headlamps benevolent beside red ranks of ordinary double-deckers. At their peak, Routemasters were driven by patient, proud men, a legion of good motoring exemplars, perceived to be our knights of the road.

Years later, the worst road rage I ever experienced happened when one of their descendants nearly crushed a pavement of pedestrians with his new bendy-bus, studded with Oyster Card technology. Dragging this awkward python behind him across a mini-roundabout near Lambeth Bridge, his fury was stoked, I think, by the fact that he had to do all of this on his own.

It was not always so, and was not meant to be. When I made my journeys to school, twice a day, aged five to eighteen, each one was partly on a Routemaster driven by a man in an isolated cab. He was free to concentrate on the road, while the interior was managed by a man or woman looking after the welfare of the passengers on the top and bottom decks. These bus conductors, with leather cash bags swinging by their sides, did a proper job. The way they ran a bus gave it a personality, and their ability to communicate with thousands of daily travellers was an important lubricant in the cold machine of London life. I am indebted to London's bus conductors, not because I ever skipped a fare, which seemed impossible on a two-man bus, but because it was through them that I encountered my first person without a Judeo-Christian background.

My bus to primary school from our house on Bromley Common was the number 47, and it carried me four stops up the A21. The regular conductor was called Charlie and he delivered a sparkling line in patter. 'Hold tight, now. Romantics upstairs. Rheumatics downstairs,' and so on. Charlie was a bottom-of-the-bill music-hall turn who'd croon a snatch of Matt Monro, also a busman, and say, 'Who's that singing? Do leave off. Lady down here's just had her ears syringed. You all right, duck? I say, YOU ALL RIGHT?'

One morning it had been raining at the bus stop and I jumped aboard damply, taking my place on the bench seat nearest the conductor's billet, with my legs dangling. The conductor was upstairs, but I heard his ding-ding on the bell instructing the driver to move on. I had my thruppenny bit ready to pay and heard his footsteps coming down the staircase. It couldn't be Charlie, who descended gingerly and only when the bus was halted. These were the steps of a younger man, quicker, lighter, almost military.

First I saw his highly polished black shoes (Charlie's were scuffed, and sometimes he even wore open-toed sandals). Then I saw the shining buttons on his jacket, and his lapels flashing like mirrors with assorted badges of honour for service to London Transport. Finally I saw his beard and turban and nearly jumped out of my skin. Who or what was this?

'Fare, please,' he said to me, and I offered my open hand instantly. Charlie would slowly turn the crank handle on his ticket machine as if it hadn't been oiled since the war. Mr Singh span his handle like lightning, tearing my ticket and putting it into my palm before I realised I'd paid him.

'Any more fare, please,' he said, walking up the aisle towards the front, allowing me to gaze at him in awe. He wore his uniform like a regimental officer, straight-backed and proud. His turban was jet black, and when he turned towards me I averted my eyes from his. They seemed to flash darkly. I was like an ignorant young Kipling meeting an unfamiliar type for the first time in the Punjab. I was terrified.

When I got off the bus outside school on Masons Hill, I walked towards the gate and was shocked to see that the man driving was wearing a turban as well. The driver's cab was an anonymous position, usually, its occupant more likely than the conductor to have tie undone, fag lit and jacket slung over the seat. This driver looked like he was in the main tank position approaching the Khyber Pass.

My teacher that year was Mrs Warren, a rare import from America whose flower-power miniskirts would levitate to display her equally lush knickers when she rubbed the top of the black-board. In most matters she was more a woman of the world than any other teacher, with a whiff of Haight Ashbury in her hair, but in answer to my question, Mrs Warren knew only enough to inform me that Mr Singh was probably a Sikh, which sounded to me like he was a spy looking for a lost ruby or something. I asked why he had a bandage on his head and she said it was called a turban. I asked why he wore a turban and she explained that it was because Sikh men didn't cut their hair or beards. I asked why, and she started a lesson on long division.

I asked Betty after school if she knew, but multiculturalism figured on her agenda somewhere between paying the window cleaner every other month and painting the house every decade. She'd seen Sikhs, of course, and in her view some of the more mature lady Sikhs with their exposed spare tyres might have done everyone a favour by covering up; but each to their own, and certainly the menfolk looked pretty handsome. I couldn't have known that Sikhs had featured in many films she'd seen in her own childhood – usually brave, monosyllabic fighters or occasionally devious vil-lains not Sikhs at all but non-specified Hindus or Muslims whose Indian subcontinent identity was signified by a turban.

This was ironic. Tradition said that the first Sikh, Guru Nanak, living at the same time as Henry VIII, had heard the voice of God when bathing in a stream and returned, saying, 'There is no Hindu; there is no Muslim.' So began a life of wandering. Once, Nanak was scolded by a mullah for falling asleep with his feet pointing towards Mecca.

Nanak replied, 'Then turn my feet in a direction where God is not.'

His thinking laid the foundation for nine more gurus who followed him until Sikhism had fully evolved with the Tenth Guru, Gobind Singh, known as Padshah (Tenth Emperor). What had developed by 1699 drew on a number of threads in Indian religion, identifying Sikhs as distinct from Hindus and Muslims by the turban, and allying Punjabi castes such as the *jats*, who were farmers, with merchants, who believed in devotion or *bhakti*.

So as to break down caste barriers, Gobind Singh encouraged Sikhs to drink *amrit* or nectar from a common bowl, and his legacy was the definitive Sikh sacred book, a gathering of accumulated texts, the Guru Granth. It is this book which is the Sikh's living, eleventh guru.

My daughter showed me this as part of her RE homework. She'd made a cardboard *Gurudwara* (Guru House) where this book was the central feature, just as it had always been at the Sikh's holiest shrine, the Golden Temple in Amritsar. Sikhism has some refreshingly clear aspects for children studying multi-faith society. It has, for example, an evocative, clubbable code of things which must be worn if you are to be one of the *Khalsa*, the 'pure ones'. *Khalsa* men have to wear the Five Ks, which stand for *Kesh* (uncut hair and beard), *Kirpan* (a dagger), *Kanga* (a comb), *Kachhera* (breeches or shorts) and *Kara* (a steel bangle).

I'd like to ask Mr Singh now what he'd thought of George Harrison's 'Within You Without You', and I'd also want to find out how he observed the five Ks whilst wearing a London Transport uniform. Hair, beard, comb and bangle must have been easy enough. He certainly never wore breeches, but he might have had long-johns under his trousers, I suppose. If he had a dagger it was not on display, and would have been illegal. Perhaps he had a Swiss Army penknife in his pocket.

By the time I encountered the one other key identifier of Sikhism – that the Guru Granth required all men to be called Singh (lion) and all women Kaur (princess) – the London Sikhs had moved up a notch. This dawned on me when London Transport printed a complete list of newsagents where one could buy a new invention called the Travelcard. This poster was plastered on bus shelters when I was doing my O levels and I was astonished that, though there were a few Smiths and the odd Jones, more than half were called Singh. This was mystifying to us ignoramuses of London town who assumed either that there was one very fertile family, or that a newsagent caste in India had performed a brilliant reverse takeover on their former imperial rulers.

On thousands of my childhood bus journeys, Mr Singh the bus conductor remained a powerful figure. His aura suggested that if Clint Eastwood had been Indian he would have been a Sikh, yet beneath his patriarchal exterior he was plainly a gentle man. This became manifest on the worst day of my primary school life. We had moved house three miles south by then, and so my bus trip was longer and potentially quite fraught, as it was crowded and not always easy to get on.

One day, the six o' clock news said that a man called Sid had ordered his comrades to inflict yet another railway strike on an exhausted nation. He was aiming for parity with astronauts. Passing resolutions and calling them Days of Action later guaranteed Margaret Thatcher twelve years as Prime Minister. The effect on a small boy travelling on his own on a strike day was to be cast amongst an additional heaving horde of train-goers slumming it on the bus and groaning about it being like a tin of bloody sardines.

I was just about able to struggle on board the 47, but unfortunately when it came to my stop I couldn't get off. I was a bit of a tough nut on the quiet and not given to behaving like a cissy, but I was stuck at the front of the bus with thirty people blocking my exit and unable to reach the bell-cord on the ceiling. The next two stops were 'request' only, so the driver with his full load sailed though them. I had overshot school by about a mile. I didn't panic, but I was silently crying in distress, which eventually came to the attention of a lady in a hat.

'Conductor,' she barked, and I saw Mr Singh's anxious face appearing above the heads of the sardines. Swiftly he tugged three times on the bell, brought the bus to a stop, and made his way through the passengers. As I approached the open deck at the back I was still crying. I would be late for school for the first time ever, I didn't know how to get back there, and I didn't have any spare money to do so. I prepared to step on to the pavement alone, but I felt Mr Singh's hand on my shoulder.

'Wait, sir, please.'

He stepped out into the traffic and across the road. Like the lion of his good name, he stood in the way of a 47 approaching from the other direction, bringing it to an unscheduled halt. He came back, guided me across, and set me at the back of this bus at the conductor's billet. On Mr Singh's authority I travelled back free of charge.

I saw him a few days later, but we never spoke of it. In fact, all he ever said to me was what he said on day one: 'Fare, please'. More impressively, he didn't hint at any familiarity. What meant most to him was not what a more slippery individual would have liked, my gratitude, but that in accordance with his honourable beliefs we had both retained our pride.

All of which has made me feel a deal of sympathy for Sikhs. In 1984, I was appalled when their Golden Temple was mortar-bombed by Mrs Gandhi's government, for which she lost her life when one of her own Sikh bodyguards retaliated and shot her. I felt guilty, too, that both Hindu nationalism and Sikh separatism were part of the backwash of Empire. We had buggered off in 1947, at the polite request of Gandhi, leaving the small matter of the creation of the separate Hindu India and Muslim Pakistan and

Bangladesh. Hundreds of thousands were slaughtered during Partition, and the later truce came at the price of sweeping the issue of the Sikh home state, Kashmir, under a diplomatic carpet.

My high estimation of British Sikhs led me to be unforgivably rude to one outside the Imperial Hotel in Delhi years later. I was on business there for a few days, accompanied by a female colleague. One afternoon I walked out of the hotel precincts on to a dusty main street of three-wheelers beating out the rhythm of Indian traffic on their horns in the intense heat. I tried not to breathe too deeply and headed for a meeting at the British Council, but before I had walked fifty yards I was seized upon by a tall Sikh, to whom I felt, as ever, well inclined. He gave me his card and I imagined he wanted an introduction to someone in the embassy or a similar favour. He then declared himself to be an astrologer.

'Sir, I see you are a very great man. You are here with a woman who is not your wife and you love her very much.'

I looked up into his eyes. They were redder than Mr Singh's. Some of his teeth were gold too.

'It is important that I make an astrological chart for you, sir, so that you may make a propitious choice.'

I stroked my chin crossly.

'I'm sorry, I don't believe in astrology.'

'But there are forces in play concerning your greatness which I will enable you to understand. Twenty dollars only. We may sit over here.'

He had two foldaway chairs set against the high boundary wall of the hotel, an outdoor consulting room.

'No thank you.'

'If you do not follow my advice, sir, it would be very bad.'

My mouth pursed into an angry O, emitting an infuriated puff of air. The poor fellow had just located my tender button marked charlatan, yet playing deep in my unconscious was the memory of Mr Singh. I wanted to get away from this con man, but out of respect for Mr Singh I felt bound to say why.

'I'm sorry, and this might seem harsh,' I began,' but what's happened here is that you've been watching my hotel, you've seen me with this woman, and you are having a punt that we're having an affair. We are not. At home, I have a wife and four children, and, to be quite frank, your approaching me with your mumbo-jumbo like this is an insult to all of them.'

'No, no.'

'Yes, yes. You know astrology is untrue and so do I, so please don't try to con me.'

And with that I had gone much, much too far.

'No, sir, you must not say that.'

His face had fallen. I had forgotten how Mr Singh had shown me respect and been most careful to leave me with my pride. For what had seemed, a few moments earlier, like sound reasons I'd made hateful if accurate accusations against this man for which he had no response. I'd taken away his pride.

If that was not bad enough, I felt as if I had declared myself a typically hard-hearted believer in nothing from the northern hemisphere, making a frightening spectacle for a man who probably fully believed in what he was saying. I realised that if I tried now to explain to him that I was not entirely without belief, it could only worsen the encounter.

'I'm sorry,' I said, and walked away, reddening with shame. I walked until he could not see me, and turned back to look. He was leaning against a tree, stupefied, shaking his head. I must have seemed like a malign white djinn who had emerged from the hotel and bitten him.

'Oh, Christ,' I said out loud, 'what have I done?'

An answer was not forthcoming.

Good Evans

In September 1970, aged almost nine, I arrived at a school in the genteel south London suburb of Dulwich where I was to be educated for the next nine years. This was Big School, and made Miss Edan seem a very long time ago. The spiritual matters I soon encountered consisted of a series of forearm smashes delivered from a more turbulent world than I'd imagined could exist.

I was already vulnerable. That summer had seen my disillusionment in what many teachers regarded as a more important constituent of moral fibre than my religion – my sense of being English. In July 1970 the England football team had travelled to the World Cup in Mexico as reigning champions – real men, winners cut from our nation's finest cloth. I had been too young for the 1966 World Cup, but in 1970, with my ninth birthday looming and new satellite technology beaming the games on to our black and white TV, I was a passionate fan. I was a believer.

What happened next was my first experience of visceral disappointment, of raw defeat putting my loss of fairyland in the shade. (If I'd known then that it foretold yet more failure, that England wouldn't even qualify for the tournaments in 1974 or 1978, I'm not sure what I'd have thought. Was it credible that I'd spend my entire school career without our troubling the scorers at a competition we should have been winning?) As I arrived at big school, all I knew was that we'd been two-nil up in a Mexican quarter-final against West Germany and managed to get ourselves knocked out two-three.

This was not meant to be. All year I'd collected my World Cup coins from the Esso station opposite Bromley bus garage. I'd persuaded my father to buy his petrol there rather than the more convenient Mobil garage in Locks Bottom to enable this, causing my mother to forfeit free glass tumblers, china mugs and Green Shield stamps just so that I could press these coins into a cardboard display frame bearing the Three Lions crest. I'd saved and traded my way to a complete set a month before the World Cup started, with an odd surplus of Brian Labones and Norman Hunters. With my display frame facing outwards from my window sill for the world to see, I began that summer feeling part of the greatest nation in the world.

When I entered Dulwich a few weeks later I'd learned, with millions of other wide-eyed children, that if there is one thing you should never believe in too fervently, it is national destiny. We had lost. The adult world seemed to move on (our sporting press in those days still retained some perspective), but for us smaller ones it felt like disaster, a Dunkirk of the spirit.

It didn't help my progress that my morale on entering Dulwich was already shaky. The headmaster of my primary school had made a little speech in front of the school bidding me farewell at the end of the previous term. I was leaving early and there was a bit of an edge in his comments. I was about to learn, he said, how it would feel not to be a shark in a goldfish bowl but a minnow in the ocean. He'd given me a book prize every year for the previous half-decade, so this sudden lack of faith in my ability to transfer any brain skills learned at his establishment was a shock to my self-confidence. The question was, he frowned, would I still be able to swim?

The simple answer, in the literal sense, was that I could not swim at all. When we were forced into the freezing pool at Dulwich on day two I was left splashing about in the shallows while other superhuman boys from something called 'The Prep' thrashed their way to the deep end. Not to worry, I thought, I'll catch up, but when I emerged up the steps I was lined up against a wall with all the other non-swimmers and told that in future classes I would have to wear a pair of white trunks over the ones I had on, the aquatic equivalent of the dunce's cap. Religious life is full of such stigma, from the Mark of Cain onwards. Cain's scar was given him to ensure that nobody slew him for murdering his brother Abel. He had to suffer guilt. If he'd been forced into these white trunks, designed like a saucy bikini, white panels fore and aft secured with string at the sides, he'd have died of shame.

Sport was full of such incongruities. In our first rugby lesson, while boys from 'The Prep' scooted about like Barry John, I learned that this game was played with an oval ball which didn't bounce properly, that you had to throw it backwards at all times, and that, no, we didn't play soccer here. Ever. Perplexingly, wide-hipped rugby teachers insisted that their throwy-backy sport was called 'football'. Still grieving after the events of Mexico, I began to feel as if the great game itself was being subsumed by idiots, big ones with loud voices.

The strangeness took a firmer hold as my first days turned into weeks. Art lessons were run by a pernickety man who rendered me scared to put paint to paper for fear of his acid judgements. At primary school we had self-expressed. Under his camp eye, any child not likely to exhibit at the Royal Academy was only good for washing the paint pots. One of my first efforts, a self-portrait in profile, was derided for not having ears. I burned with shame, self-conscious that my ears were bigger than I would have liked; their absence from the side of my painted head drew even more attention to the fact. It is forgotten now that many of us had a thing about our ears after we'd seen our future king's investiture as the Prince of Wales at Harlech Castle with flappers like Dumbo. Absurdly concerned that we should not look like him, we longed for pin-prick ears, the lugholes of a dolphin.

Stranger still were the morning assemblies run by a truly terrifying lower school head teacher who'd tell us stories which chill me to this day. He was a fat little chap but he buzzed through our lines with his black gown billowing like a mean-minded fly. We simply never knew which direction he was going in next. One morning, when I was feeling especially small and unhappy and wondering how I had ended up in a school with 1,500 pupils from a school of 150, he barked at us that in his rightful judgement we were not sufficiently grateful for the privileged lives we led. With thumbs hooked into his waistcoat pockets and his podgy pink lower lip jutting and glistening, he told us that the day before he had visited an unfortunate boy from another school in hospital. The poor lad had developed a tumour in one of his limbs, he said. I didn't know what a tumour was, but what followed left me in no doubt that it was bad.

'The growth of this boy's tumour eventually necessitated the amputation of his leg.'

We blanched.

'The type of amputation in his case is known as the full hind-quarter removal.'

He paused. I felt sick.

'For those of you who do not realise this,' he embellished, and this would have been all one hundred per cent of those aged nine to twelve enjoying his anecdote, 'the full hind-quarter section involves amputation of the leg above and below the knee and the removal of the entire buttock.'

The use of the word buttock left many of us not knowing how the hell we were meant to respond. But the story had already had its punch line and he was ready to move on with the assembly as if he'd just read out a change of arrangement for PE.

'We'll sing number 83, "Now Thank We All Our God".'

I remember fumbling for the right page, (it was an offence to take too long), and, while his cold blue eyes scanned our hearts and hands and voices, thinking, what the hell is wrong with you, man?

Buttock removal was just the beginning. Other favourite morning pick-me-ups involved young boys he'd read about in the *Telegraph* who had fallen on to iron railings from trees. He rolled 'impale' around his jowls with all the savour he had taken in 'amputate'. If what he wanted to do was scare our young minds witless and prime our fear of the potential horrors lurking for us in the big, wide world, he'd done his job.

Unfortunately it also fell to him to give us military-style instruction in how to pray. At St George's and at primary school, this was a straightforward matter of pressing the palms of the hands together with the tips of the fingers pointing skywards. Thus, with podgy mitts set fair like a church steeple, I would communicate with my maker.

This would not do for a senior school chap. At my first morning assembly at Dulwich the head teacher trumpeted, 'Let us pray' and then yelled, '*No! Not like that!*'

Our tiny hands were frozen, while older boys who'd been through this the year before openly laughed at our callowness.

'*Shut up,*' he screamed at them, and then showed us how we had to press the forefinger of the right hand to our left temple, the thumb of the right hand to the right temple, and support the elbow of our right arm in the palm of our left hands. I hope you're trying this at home.

'I want to see it like that every morning. Now, let us pray. Dear Lord, we thank thee for thy eternal beneficence, for sparing us from punishment even when we have done wrong . . .' He'd then scan the sea of bowed heads to note any twitching with guilt . . . 'and give thanks for the work of this school.'

The work of the school. This was even more confusing, along with the odd prayer position and the continuing absence of any mention of Jesus. It was absolutely understood that when he yelled 'Dear Lord' he was addressing the organ grinder, not the useless son who got himself killed. But the school itself, though called Dulwich College, had another name: Alleyn's College of God's Gift.

There was little modesty in this. First, there was a perfectly good school a mile away called Alleyn's which would have had good reason to think it tactless for its big brother to go round trading partly under the same name. Second, God's gift? This was how my mother's newspaper described sexual vanity. 'Humperdinck thinks he's God's gift,' Jean Rook would write. 'Well, please release me, Engelbert.'

What was even more confusing was that Edward Alleyn, the man who had founded the original school for sixteen poor scholars four hundred years earlier, was never mentioned. There was a Founder's Day in early July, and a blue cornflower was worn to mark it. But in seventies London, even after the alleged sexual revolution, it was not thought seemly to dwell on how Alleyn had earned the fortune he then gave away. Elsewhere, his role acting alongside Shakespeare and speaking his words would have been a matter of as much pride as the decaying boat in the grounds which Ernest Shackelton had used to survive in Antarctica. Shack was hardly ever off the more boring teachers' lips. Alleyn, on the other hand, was not really one of us. Indeed, there was a suspicion that he might occasionally have been, in the parlance of *The Two Ronnies*, 'one of them'.

He was certainly a lurid theatrical type, a known master of bear-baiting, a brothel-keeper, and a wayward husband to the daughter of metaphysical poet John Donne. The assumption was that Alleyn made such a huge bequest at his death because he dreaded his monumental charge-sheet at the Pearly Gates. It was his theatrical troupe, the Admiral's Men, who were alleged to have conjured up the devil when performing Marlowe's *Dr Faustus* on tour at the Seven Stars Inn in Heavitree on the outskirts of Exeter. '*Veni, Veni, Mephistophile,*' they incanted, and suddenly twelve prancing actors became thirteen, leading to the complete disintegration of any remaining moral fibre in the company, which never performed the play again. How I would have adored knowing that the school had its origins in such richness, that there was more in its marrow than Dulwich Village and its then epically dull art gallery. These days I understand the school is rather cooler, in the modern sense, about Alleyn than it was then, especially after Ben Affleck played him in *Shakespeare In Love*.

There is real art in appointing a form teacher to induct the youngest class in a large school, and in that I was very lucky. As a parent you hope your little one will be taking their first senior step under the guidance of someone inspiring and benign, but you worry the teacher has been alloted to teach the most junior pupils because they are new to their profession.

My first form teacher at Dulwich, Mr Evans, was not new. He was a genius, a communicator and enthusiast without peer who we adored and, strangely for children so young, understood. Somehow we intuited from the outset that his occasional lapse into molten red-faced temper was so far off any normal scale that it was more directed at himself than any identifiable victim. We knew he only really meant it once, when he lifted a boy called Chowdrey and the desk in which he sat and threw them both skidding across the floor into a radiator. We were behind Mr Evans every inch of the way as Chowdrey span across the room, because he'd belatedly discovered what we had known for three terms – that every excuse Chowdrey had offered for not bringing his homework to school was a spectacular lie. He'd boasted about this to us without realising that only honour amongst thieves stopped us telling Mr Evans. In our eyes, he was guilty of deceiving and making a fool of a loveable and generous old man, and also implicating us in his treachery over most of a year.

Schools are not places where you can keep personality traits secret. A teacher is on constant display. Form JC clocked quite quickly that at lunchtimes Mr Evans didn't hang about in the school grounds but headed off in the direction of the nearby pub, the Alleyn's Head. Just as we were summoned by a bell to regroup for the afternoon, he was spotted walking briskly back past the pavilion towards the school with a brown paper bag shaped like a bottle jutting from his jacket pocket. Given the nature of what it was he had to teach us in that first year, it is possible that even the best of us would have resorted to a mental anaesthetic. We may have been small, but his job he was to teach us absolutely everything which would ever matter for the rest of our lives. The pressure on him and his conscience must have been enormous.

In his mathematics lessons he taught with such elegance and patience that even I understood. I marked out a football pitch the other day using Pythagoras's theorem to make the corners, and thought warmly of Mr Evans's arithmetic, though in truth, other than percentages on my VAT return, it's the only use I've had for it in many decades. Maths was not his only subject. Mr Evans also taught us Religious Education. He appreciated that few of us had been grounded in the basics of the Old Testament, as I had been at St George's and elsewhere, so he took us through it all again as if it were an historical document revealing the facts concerning the creation of the first men on Earth. In clouds of chalk dust he brilliantly dashed off multicoloured maps on the blackboard, rivalling the best pavement art in the world, and showed, in different shades, the rivers Tigris and Euphrates flowing into the Persian Gulf, how to find Babylon and Ur, and which part of Mesopotamia might have been the real Garden of Eden. He introduced us to Jerusalem, and showed us Mount Sinai, where Moses received something called the Ten Commandments, the contents of which, along with the existence of the New Testament, we did not dwell on.

In the playground after these lessons we'd ape David and Goliath, and, if it was the season, we'd sling conkers at each other on strings. We imagined what it would have been like to be Daniel in the Lions' Den, and resolved that in accordance with the fashion of the time we'd try to keep our hair reasonably long if, as the Bible said, Samson had lost all his strength after a haircut. That his savage crop had been inflicted by Delilah resonated only in the sense that Tom Jones sang a song of that name, soon to be covered deliriously by the Sensational Alex Harvey Band. We knew nothing of temptresses, and didn't have the equipment to understand that the Bible was full of them, from the Queen of Sheba to Salome.

Perhaps Mr Evans himself had once had a Delilah in his life, but if so her memory was long occluded behind billowing pipe smoke, which kept his brilliant mind sharp. Teaching mathematics plainly came easily to him, but teaching RE must have had him reaching into the brown paper bag, because the other subject he was commissioned to introduce us to would absolutely destroy the credibility of everything he had told us in RE. That subject was science.

You might not have marked Mr Evans down as a scientist. He looked like, and further up the school occasionally was, a classics teacher, his appearance perfect for playing Mr Chipping in any am-dram *Goodbye, Mr. Chips* – tweed jacket, shiny trousers with turn-ups, round tortoiseshell spectacles, a thick H.G. Wells moustache falling over his top lip, bald pate shining like a red traffic light when his temper overcame him.

In his science lessons Mr Evans shared with us his true passions. The first was the geology of the Earth, a subject with the potential to bore young minds but which in his hands was a gripping narrative of how we might go to the Dakotas or to China or our own Lyme Regis and find fossils representing millions of years of life, from ammonite to Ichthyosaur, Tyrannosaurus Rex to the Woolly Mammoth. He chalked images of these creatures on to the blackboard as passionately as a Neolithic man in a Dordogne cave, until one day one of our number asked the inevitable question.

'But sir, you said the Bible says the world is only six or seven thousand years old.'

Mr Evans had a way of raising his top lip when challenged so that his moustache tickled the end of his nose.

'I did say that. However, the evidence may tell a rather different story. On this, boys, you must eventually make up your own minds. All I can advise you is that either the biblical or the geological timeline is incorrect. They cannot both be true.'

His brown eyes beamed at us indulgently and we adored him. He was giving us our first bite at the Tree of Knowledge, but unlike the serpent he wished us only well.

His second passion, the alpha and omega of his life, was astronomy. With the Apollo moon landing of the year before, his subject had been transformed from the hobby of lonely men with thermos flasks squinting at the night sky to the prime topic of the day. The discovery of astronomy had affected his young life just as geology had changed our perspective on the Bible, though to explain this he had to share some of the straw dolls of his own childhood.

He had once been credulous too, not foolish enough to believe that there was a man in the moon or that it was made of cheese, but pretty certain that what he was seeing through his junior telescope were roads and canals running across Mars which promised a lively and possibly threatening civilisation of little green men. Further, this telescope showed him that his planet was part of a solar system which was part of a galaxy – far-fetched and challenging to his young mind but thought to be the full extent of things.

Fifty years on he was able to enlighten us rather more. Even then it was only with the shots of the blue planet from outer space that we believed with certainty that this flat thing we played on was in fact a globe inside which, defying all reason, a molten core created enough gravity to prevent us floating off into the sky. This alone had begged some questions for any of us inclined to entertain the possibility of a literal God, a creator of the Earth. Had he created the rest of the solar system too? The galaxy? If so – a crucial concern in a childish mind – where did he live and, when we'd already considered how busy he must have been listening to all the prayers on Earth and then pulling the right strings, was he also God of the galaxy too? How could he possibly find the time to fit it all in?

Mr Evans took us beyond the solar system and the galaxy. He had news for us of something called the universe. What was more, this universe had once been packed into something the size of a full stop, had exploded at the beginning of time, and was still expanding outwards on an infinite scale. Our brains began to hurt.

Then he began to explain that when we looked up at the sky we could indeed see stars like our own sun with the naked eye, but what we were looking at was that star as it had been when dinosaurs ruled the earth. It took that long for the light from those stars to reach us. Every night from our bedroom windows we were looking through both space and time. Maybe the light from the nearest star had set off when Julius Caesar was being murdered on the steps of the Forum – to which Mr Evans added that we might be sitting in our classrooms inhaling a molecule of Caesar's dying breath, since the atmosphere of the Earth was finite and constantly recycled. (In this he'd skipped ahead. We hadn't realised Caesar had been murdered. We'd thought his life had revolved around Londonium.) Across the curriculum Mr Evans was like a Starman who didn't think he'd blow our minds, but he did.

It seems likely that even the dimmest of class JC saw the implication of the clash between the Bible and geology in the matter of Creation; but it would take a pretty smart nine-year-old to keep up with Mr Evans when it came to the wider implications of living in a changing universe. One such child was Michael Burton, a red-haired freckly boy originally from Australia, whose treble tone rose at the end of each sentence.

'Sir, is the universe still expanding?'

'Yes, Burton, it is.'

'Sir, will it stop expanding one day, or will it carry on for ever?'

'We don't know that, Burton, but it seems likely that the expansion must eventually stop. When, I am unable to say.'

'Sir.'

'Burton.'

'Sir, if there's gravity everywhere in the universe, like there is here on Earth, what will happen when the universe stops getting bigger? Won't all the gravity make it shrink again?'

'Yes, Burton, I'd imagine it would.'

'Won't that squash us, sir?'

'It might, lad, but we needn't worry about that.'

We all exhaled with relief.

'Because, as you recall, the sun is essentially a ball of gas, mainly hydrogen and helium, which will eventually burn itself out. When that happens, I'm afraid our solar system has had it anyway.'

The classroom was silent as we processed this nugget. As one it hit us that this was not good news.

'Sir,' we chorused, our tiny minds filled with fear of this imminent event.

'Now, you mustn't lose sleep over this, boys,' Mr Evans went on, pushing his spectacles back up his nose, 'because that will be in hundreds of millions of years time, and, to be frank, I doubt very much that any of us will be here to worry about it.'

It was my turn, always a loyal advocate for the species.

'When the world ends, will there still be men anyway, sir?'

'I don't know, Arnott.'

He was telling us the truth, but he was also telling a group of nine-year-olds, many of whom, like me, still nursed what we considered realistic ambitions to be immortal, that even if we were, our planet wasn't. I wonder now if that lesson was the one which set me on a course entertaining doubt and faith in equal measure, forever after a fascinated defender of both.

Whatever the truth, it is clear that as boys we reacted in different ways. Michael Burton had been my best friend in that first year. His father was a senior meteorologist at the Met Office in London. For the first two terms, Michael and I were out on our own at the top of the class, but somehow I just didn't have the academic legs. Puberty began early for me, and the arrival of mysterious hairs was a major distraction from abstractly studying natural sciences. I seemed to be turning into King Kong myself.

Michael pressed on, though. At lunchtimes he played for a while, but then retreated to the junior library to read nourishing magazines such as *Look and Learn* and *World of Wonder*. The only magazine I could be found with at lunchtime was *Health and Efficiency*, which was shared with us all by the son of a renowned clergyman, Canon Paul Oestreicher. The impact of seeing all those bosoms and bums bouncing quite knocked the Theory of Relativity out of my head. Michael had tried the *Reader's Digest* version on me one afternoon at his house, but it would be thirty more years before my pulse slowed enough to try to understand it again.

Michael Burton reacted another way. He accepted the truth of what he was being told, studied more, spoke to his scientist parents, went to Cambridge, and is now a Professor of Astronomy back in Australia, where he scans deep space for molecules of this and that associated with the formation of new stars. Maybe he's hoping for a planet we can all move to one day.

I failed O level Physics in the end. But I am not entirely stupid. Perhaps the way Michael and I took diverging paths after the revelations of Mr Evans can be accounted for elsewhere. My father had done his best to at least ground me in the Judeo-Christian tradition which underpinned so much of my country's history. He didn't know what to believe and nor did I, but we would both have agreed that the questions mattered.

Michael Burton's parents, however, already had a raft of ideas about the world entirely worked out. They had a living room their children were never allowed to enter. They did not allow their sons to eat South African produce, and the look on my mother's face when she offered Michael an orange and he said 'Is it *Outspan*? Because I don't eat South African fruit' was priceless. Above all, they were the first people I ever met who proclaimed loudly and with utter certainty that their family were not interested in God, the many churches within a mile of their house, the Christmas message from the Archbishop of Canterbury or the latest Bull from the Pope. For they, Mr and Mrs Burton, Michael and Tony, were something called Atheists.

Yaba-Daba-Doo

For a family like the Burtons to proclaim itself atheist in the seventies involved a small measure of courage, like wanting to ban the bomb or adopting vegetarianism, but at the same time it went unremarked. A statement of atheism lacked impact, and, worse, it lacked power. This was odd, because the opposition was flat on the floor after more than a century of body-blows. Logically, atheists should have finished mainstream religion off ages ago. The lay philosopher's defence of religion in an evolutionary world is why, if it had no survival value, would it still exist? There should have been no reason for Michael to sit out assembly with other non-adherents to Anglicanism. That assembly ought to have been long abolished, replaced by a humanist gathering.

Mainstream entertainment of the time could have done no more to help. The character of the British priest was lampooned for the pleasure of millions on a scale which made Hogarth seem respectful: Derek Nimmo's feeble vicar in *All Gas and Gaiters*, the limp His Reverence in *Dad's Army*, testy Father O'Hara in *Some Mothers Do 'Ave 'Em*, the buck-toothed berk of the *Dick Emery Show*. Worse, when Ken Russell cast Oliver Reed as a priest in *The Devils* he wasn't planning a performance in the mold of G.K. Chesterton's detective *Father Brown*. This was to be tits and bums and burnings and lashings of ketchup blood.

There was more ketchup when Patrick Troughton was pierced by a church spire in *The Omen*, one of the first in a line of priests warning of imminent events prophesied by the Book of Revelations. This kind of figure was worse than the funny ones: he was mad, obsessed, full of hocus-pocus. King of all priest lampooners was the Irish comedian *Dave Allen*, decades before *Father Ted*, who took every rite of the Catholic Church and defiled it, from baptism to cremation. Most Britons weren't Catholic, but his sacrilege spoke for generations who couldn't understand why they still had any form of religion inflicted on them at all.

Even when the churches tried to engage through mainstream media their efforts were risible. Jess Yates at his organ on ITV's *Stars On Sunday*, reading out letters from widows and playing along with their favourite hymns, was like a protracted sketch by Alan Bennett. As was the BBC's *Songs of Praise*, but when it came to record at Bromley Parish church, the fight for tickets was fiercer than for Sinatra's comeback concert. We watched the transmission at home months later, seeing faces we knew had not been inside a church for years decked out in new hats and dresses from Medhursts. We laughed, but it felt a little too much like laughing at the temple being overrun by the money lenders. Where was the truth in any of this?

Not on *Thought for the Day* on Radio Four, which served mainly to expose how much priests depended on the headlines for their sermons, a habit which seemed hysterically funny when magnified by the airwaves. 'We've all been affected by the miners' strike this week, many spending evenings in the dark. Yet we are not alone. Let us not forget that after God made the universe and the oceans, it was he who said "Let There Be Light".' Second-guessing the current affairs hook in the day's broadcast was a game many would play.

The established churches seemed to have lost any facility for communicating with their potential flock, yet the atheists' message wasn't getting through either. Negative propositions are notoriously hard to sell, though latterly Professor Dawkins has proved this publishing maxim wrong, along with the one about not selling a book with the word God in the title. Ironically, he and his publishers have grown rich defying both with *The God Delusion*. But it took a century for this to happen.

The difficulty for atheists was that the sensational world news they had made, the kind which changed civilisation, had come more than a hundred years before. We can be certain it was sensational then because the finest weathervane in the history of British journalism, Charles Dickens, stitched a line about the fad of the day into *Bleak House* in 1852: 'Implacable November weather. As much mud in the streets as if the waters had but newly retired from the face of the earth, and would it not be wonderful to meet a Megalosaurus, forty feet long or so waddling like an elephantine lizard up Holborn Hill?' His reference to the waters over the earth was diabolically clever, because a series of recent discoveries had rendered absurd the standard claim that the Earth was, according to the inspired guess of biblical scholars, about six thousand years old. Dinosaurs were but the latest and greatest proof that this could not be true, and neither was it tenable to insist, as some priests still did, that they had been wiped out by Noah's flood and their bodies left in the ancient mud.

This turned into the most wonderfully florid controversy, filled with sparkling and often tragic characters. A few miles from where I now live, Mary Anning uncovered the first complete skeleton of an Ichthyosaur in 1811 beneath Black Ven cliff, between Lyme Regis and Charmouth. A young teenager, she helped her family's meagre income by selling fossils, though nobody knew what they were. Ammonites were referred to as sea snakes, and pieces of larger creatures were thought to be from crocodiles. A great admirer of her labour was William Buckland from nearby Axminster, a geologist of great integrity who wrestled for decades to make the fossil record and the Bible compatible and was ultimately condemned to an asylum.

There was also a good guy–bad guy story in the development of the science of dinosaurs – Gideon Mantell versus Richard Owen, penniless doctor with a deformed and painful spine versus establishment man and thief of others' research. Owen prevailed, and Mantell, like Anning and Buckland, died in reduced circumstances. But Owen's hubris and insistence that he could keep geology and theology in tandem led to an intellectual crash in the most humiliating of circumstances. His ally, the Bishop of

Oxford, ended up in a no-holds-barred debate, climaxing in his withering attack on the brilliant geologist Thomas Huxley. Famously, the Bishop asked Huxley whether he was descended from a monkey through his grandfather or his grandmother. There was much chortling from the clerical benches, but Huxley trumped him. 'I would not be ashamed to have a monkey for an ancestor, but I would be ashamed to be connected with a man who used great gifts to obscure the truth.'

By the time this debate percolated down to us in Form JC, more than a century had gone by. One spring morning after assembly, Mr Evans walked us up the hill from Dulwich to the then run-down and uninspiring Horniman's Museum in Forest Hill to see bits of fossil and dinosaur vertebrae. We ate our sandwiches in the garden and then walked on to the grounds of Crystal Palace Park, where the building from the Great Exhibition of 1851 had been permanently located, only to burn down in the 1930s. All that remained of significance was a display by the lake which the dastardly Richard Owen had helped devise: life-size metal models of a huge iguanodon with its tail over the water, and a pair of pterodactyls in a rockery above.

It would be twenty years before *Jurassic Park*, but we knew these models were quite ridiculous, painted in colours which seemed to have been chosen by a poster-paint factory owner with colour blindness. In an uncomfortable way, they seemed less like honest attempts to recreate the geological past than icons of a passing battle in Victorian science, as irrelevant and tedious to us as a leaky-roofed Victorian church in the nearby suburbs.

It is a coincidence that I live on what is now known as the Jurassic Coast, Fossil Central, home to Anning and Buckland. I grew up cycling into the countryside of Downe in north-west Kent where Charles Darwin retreated after the publication of his *Origin of Species* in 1859, in which he outlined his theory of evolution by the process of natural selection. He was rewarded for his work by being caricatured as an ape, which was ironic as he was actually deeply troubled by the implication in his work that man was not made in the image of God but descended from other primates. Damned with faint praise by the jealous Richard Owen, he attracted passionate support from Thomas Huxley, and the argument was settled in Darwin's favour for ever. When I looked through the gates of Down House as a child, it did not seem a happy place. It seemed all too probable that Darwin felt crushed by the brilliance of his findings, that he wondered to the end if he wasn't right to describe himself as the Devil's chaplain.

This was the problem for atheism. Its heroes seemed either reluctant or damaged. The support from non-scientists was too often tainted by coming from lapsed believers on the verge of madness. Friedrich Nietzsche's notion of man as superman was horribly associated with the Aryan beliefs favoured by the Nazis. Freud's opposition to Nazism was heroic, but his writings described God as an illusion connected to the Oedipus complex, and in later years he wrote a number of ill-judged historical speculations on the lives of Moses and Leonardo which undermined much of his work that was not strictly specific to individual neurosis. William Blake used to walk into the Dulwich countryside from his home in Lambeth, and while he seemed unclear whether he wanted to kill God or make man God, his infection by Christianity in early life seemed to have contributed to both his genius and the delusions which fed his unique art in the *Songs of Innocence and Experience*.

There were two other reasons why the atheists kept their heads down during my childhood. First, it might be a given that they would rejoice in societies run without God, but the examples up and running shamed the very idea. Communism, as implemented in the Soviet Union and its satellites, brooked no opposition, particularly from the Church, and loud enough noises of protest reached us from behind the Iron Curtain to signal that godless societies were off to an unfortunate start. They seemed as programmable by ideas as the faithful were by beliefs. A number of our teachers swore by *Chairman Mao's Little Red Book* or

Lenin's *What Is To Be Done*, which they carried about in their pockets with all the reverence of a book of psalms.

The second reason the atheists could not put their message across was that it was already being done for them by senior church figures from Dom Cupitt to the Bishop of Durham, David Jenkins. Throughout my childhood, these two heavy-hitting theologians, whose predecessors gave Darwin such an unhappy time, finally began to talk of the Bible stories as figurative and metaphorical, to allow questions about the actual virginity of Mary or the actual ascension of Christ. This took some courage on their part, and the press stoked up little bonfires of condemnation, but they were merely catching up with the rest of us. Of course the Bible wasn't the literal truth. When Darwin and Buckland were struggling with the account scientific investigation had provided for the origin of life, there were good men in their Church who fully accepted it. They just couldn't find the right words to say so.

If only Charles Kingsley of my cherished *The Water Babies* had prevailed. Dotting romantic little defences for the inexplicable wonder of creation across his book and quoting Wordsworth, he teased scientists over the grandiosity of some of their claims on limited evidence. He knew the conventional God on a cloud was gone for ever, and in the book he painted another realm of charm and learning which gave those who needed some magic in their lives a deal of comfort. He was then what the most effective and long-lasting wing of the Church of England has evolved into now – the institutionalised acceptance of doubt.

Yet even in the seventies a hardcore movement for Jesus fought on against this, at its strongest across the Atlantic. We could feel the distant drumbeat – evangelist Billy Graham had sowed the seed a decade earlier, and Harold Webb trading as Cliff Richard continued to water it. At school there was a Christian club, who saw no gain in emulating their established superiors at the General Synod, in letting faith be degraded from absolute certainty to a waffling compromise. Their members came from newer churches in unfashionable pockets of south London. They were quietly preparing a new front and a decade later they'd be strong enough to make another pass at me.

Assembly

Atheists knew their place. Every morning from 9 a.m. until 9.20 a.m. their place was in an empty classroom finishing off some homework with the Catholics, the Jews, the Hindus, and a boy from Sri Lanka who might have been Buddhist but I suspect just enjoyed the extra time for getting his work done. The rest of us were told horror stories and yelled at by the lower school headmaster, except on Wednesdays, when Assembly was in the Great Hall and the non-attendees dithered about in the main school library underneath.

The largest group were the Catholics. Why they didn't come into Assembly with the rest of us wasn't clear. They were welcome, the hymns and prayers were the same, and there was no communion, so that would not have been an impediment. It must have felt odd: a Catholic boy wouldn't encounter a millisecond of prejudice from teachers or children, yet the history we were all taught was oozing Catholic villainy.

Once a Catholic boy called Stephen invited half a dozen of us round to a well-provided family fireworks party. After charred sausages and Tizer, his dad merrily set fire to Guy Fawkes, the Popish plotter who had tried to blow up Parliament, the celebration of whose grim execution figured on the calendar below Christmas and birthdays but in solid third place above Easter. It felt bizarre, as if a Hindu family wreathed in smiles had asked us round to fry Gandhi.

As the evening grew darker I avoided the sparklers, which had always scared me, and went to the bottom of the garden where Stephen's big brother Dave was setting off the Catherine wheels. I hadn't seen one before, whizzing around a rusty nail on a section of rotting trellis, phosphorescent and reeking of explosive powder. When it fizzled out, Dave asked us if we knew why it was called a Catherine wheel. I quite fancied a girl called Catherine Hazell, which entertained the group for a few moments, but that was as far as my learned contribution was going to take us.

Dave pointed to the burnt remains of the wheel and told us the gory story of a good Catholic girl from Alexandria who had refused the attentions of a Roman emperor in the fourth century and as a reward for brilliantly arguing her case before fifty philosophers was tortured on a cartwheel. Throughout her torment she had insisted she must stay true to herself, as she was a bride of Christ.

'But the wheel couldn't kill her,' said Dave, 'so they cut her head off. And the neck stump didn't spurt blood. It was something else.'

With that he walked away and set fire to four more Catherine wheels he'd nailed on the other side of the trellis facing a railway line. The sparks flew, and the night air screamed. Satisfied, he sidled to where I and another friend Paddy were now standing well back.

'What do you reckon it was?' he continued.

'What what was, Dave?'

'The stuff coming out of her neck.'

Paddy guessed giblets, but Dave scoffed.

'It was milk. What do you think about that, then?'

He nodded at us meaningfully, as if we had just been given a secret code, and in a way we had. The inaugural captain of our religious team, Henry VIII, had cauterised us Anglicans from all these amazing stories. And while Stephen's family had martyrs for every day of the year, we had none at all.

The experience the Catholics had in class might make a useful thinking point for Muslims who feel victimised today. We were told that the English Civil War was solely caused by an airy-fairy, demented Catholic monarch who believed he should rule with absolute power, answerable only to God.

In seventies Britain there was only one word for this kind of man – Charles I was a nutter, and in more eloquent terms this was what we were taught.

Taking sides with the nutter, we learned, were the Catholics, who, again from our perspective were posh, rich, idle landowners and borderline fascists. When Betty and Peter very generously offered, for my tenth birthday, to take about a dozen of my friends to the Odeon Eltham to watch Richard Harris's *Cromwell*, in which a Catholic villain removed the ear of a peasant, the many-layered depiction of Charles I offered by Alec Guinness was wasted. When his head came off we in the front circle cheered, none louder than Stephen, and celebrated by throwing Maltesers on to the heads of our fellow Roundheads below. Our history curriculum hadn't taught us what Cromwell did to the Catholics next, not so much in his home country but in Ireland. We knew nothing of the clearances, the tens of thousands sent as slaves to Barbados, the destruction of a language and the banning of Catholic churches, so that priests ended up preaching in hedge schools. Even the potato famine much closer to our own times, barely one hundred years before, was never mentioned.

We understood the IRA wanted the Brits out of the north of Ireland, but we hadn't the faintest clue why, or that the bombers were indoctrinated in old grievances arising from this awful history. We didn't get it. We knew they were Catholics, but they were terrorist ones. Our own home-grown Catholics were fine, better than us in a way – they knew what they were talking about on religion, were lucky that their Pope still believed in the doctrine of transubstantiation, in a bit of mystery. The richest church I knew was the Catholic St Michael's near my house, modern brick and glass and well-heeled, with the best cars around parked outside. In other suburbs people might tell a different story of isolated Irish communities clinging to their home culture and dancing in their traditional way in community halls, but to us the Catholics were enviably coherent while we were an untutored mob.

The second largest group of abstainers from school assembly

were Jewish, and here too the matter of Roundheads and Cavaliers was relevant. By then, even though we still didn't know much about Jesus or what he was meant to mean, we were solid on our Old Testament. I had already taken against Abraham on the basis that he was prepared to kill his son for God, a serious matter. Guaranteed to raise a titter, however, was the following passage from Genesis: 'This is my covenant, which ye shall keep, between me and you and thy seed after thee; Every man child among you shall be circumcised . . . And the uncircumcised man-child whose flesh of his foreskin is not circumcised, that soul shall be cut off from his people; he hath broken the covenant.'

Here, of course, a careful tread is appropriate. Jews must be circumcised, as must Muslims (by *hadith*, handed-down teachings of Islam, but not by instruction from the Koran), and many of my schoolmates from Christian backgrounds had also lost their foreskins, but out of medical fashion. For the religious groups these are grave matters of purity and holiness. The new God of Abraham wanted to move on from human sacrifice, and the loss of a few centimetres of flesh on the eighth day of life while being given a name by a *mohel* (an observant Jew who knew how to circumcise) was, by comparison, a small price to pay.

Perhaps it is forgivable that such passages glimpsed in the Bible when we were meant to be focusing on the opposite page made us crumple with laughter. We were puerile. The very idea that Abraham's marketing strategy required thousands of adults to cut their foreskins off, and as if that was not enough, that all Egyptians were invited to do the same, seemed like something from Monty Python. Get the snip or suffer the plagues. Apparently Christians remember Jesus's first suffering at the Feast of Circumcision on 1 January, but I can't recall dancing in the streets in Bromley on New Year's Day.

The Jewish boys at Dulwich were a secular, liberal bunch. Those of us in sports teams went to away matches by coach on a Saturday morning, and if this took us via north London we'd pass through Tottenham and Stoke Newington where we'd see Orthodox Jews garbed in black with side-curls and wide-brimmed hats, moving with as little effort as possible on the *Shabbat*. Our Jews weren't remotely like that. So similar did they seem to us Christian boys that it was hard to see what all the arguments throughout history had been about.

I had a good friend, Woody, whose dad was a dentist. His house was identical to mine except for the *mezuzah* fixed on to the wooden frame of his front door containing teachings from the Torah, and the separate sinks for meat and dairy. Though I didn't know this at the time, the Torah was simply the first five books from my Bible: the Books of Genesis, Exodus, Leviticus, Numbers and Deuteronomy – the sum total of my own biblical grounding until then too.

On reflection, Woody did conform to certain stereotypes as set out by his namesake Mr Allen. He was a mine of neurotic information about things I'd have never considered – how to wash your hair to guarantee you wouldn't go bald, how many times to brush your teeth up and down at bedtime, which rock bands were essential and which were a danger to your brain. He was fabulously disdainful of anything in the charts and adored a group called *The Enid*, who he followed round the country as they played their deliberately (I assumed) uncool, pomp-orchestral performance pieces in which the singer crooned through a megaphone. I saw them with him at the Finsbury Park Rainbow once and thought they were dreadful, even their vaunted party piece, a rock *Land of Hope and Glory*. Yet no evening following *The Enid* was wasted for Woody. He was the most unlikely lady-killer, who throughout our childhoods and teenage years always managed to have a young woman on his arm, despite his bog-brush hair and zits. For Woody, it was a matter of self-belief, and these concerts were an early prototype of speed-dating.

It was Woody who broke it to me that when it came to world faiths, I was not, as I'd assumed, playing in the A team. If anything, my lot were hardly even the Bs. One summer lunchtime when we sitting against a tree in the school grounds, I asked

Woody what the beef was between Jews and Christians. I really didn't get it. Same Bible, same language. No pork chops for him, of course, but other than that what was the difference?

Woody knew. I did not. And that seemed a terrible lapse on my part after he had spoken.

'Okay,' he began, 'so you've got Jesus, yeah?'

'Yes.'

'Well, the thing my dad would say about Jesus is that, like, he was really good and clever and a nice guy and everything, but, well, sorry, he wasn't the son of God.'

'He wasn't? Who was he?'

'Don't get me wrong, he was important and, you know, you should believe in him if you want. But to my dad he's just a really important prophet.'

Woody had me at a disadvantage. I didn't know what a prophet was.

'They're all over the Bible. What Jesus did, Dad says, is take the prophesies of the coming of a Messiah one day and let everyone think it was him. He was a bit of a magician.'

My idea of a magician was Tommy Cooper or David Nixon. I tore some grass out of the ground.

'You're saying that his miracles were just tricks?'

'I don't want to offend you.'

I thought on. Maybe they were. Actually, of course they were.

'So that's what your dad thinks?'

'Yeah.'

'And you?'

'Sure.'

Woody had something else on his mind.

'The thing is, Paul, I can have this conversation with you because you're my mate. But if Dad knew we were talking about Jesus like this he'd be livid with me.'

'Why?'

'Because people like you are meant to think that people like me killed him.'

If I couldn't grasp what he meant when he was talking about prophets, I certainly didn't have the knowledge to understand where this bolt from the blue came from. It took me a while to think of any comeback.

'Yeah, but Woody, he was crucified by Pontius Pilate. He was a Roman, wasn't he?'

'All Pilate did was wash his hands of the matter. It was Herod who made it all happen.'

'He was a Roman too.'

'Christ, Paul, he was a Jewish king. And all those other guys, like the high priest Caiaphas who wanted Jesus dead, they were all Jews.'

'I see. So what did they want Jesus dead for?'

'They were scared of him. He was, like, a rebel and a blasphemer and he was going round claiming to be King of the Jews.'

Then a penny began to drop. I didn't know much about Jesus, but I'd been led to believe that he was the first Christian. It had never occurred to me – or indeed most of my friends – that he had been born a Jew.

'He was Jewish? Yes, you're right, I suppose he was.' I thought a bit longer. 'So why the heck did your lot kill him?'

Woody laughed out loud.

'There you go. You've said it. I don't believe it. Oh my God, Paul.'

So this was where the trouble had started. As children we knew about the murder of European Jews by the National Socialist Party of Germany. But how was this really for Woody? When we went to see the film of *The Odessa File* together, in which a journalist infiltrates the ranks of Nazi sympathisers in 1960s Germany, who did Woody identify with? I assumed it was Jon Voight, the good German. The character based on Simon Wiesenthal, the Jewish tracker of war criminals, was sympathetic, of course, but his role was exposition. He wasn't the kind of cool guy Woody wanted to be. Voight was.

The question, was too big for us then, so we left it alone. What was it about the Jewish people that made the Nazis murder them without a trace of conscience? I certainly couldn't answer that, and Woody didn't really want to address it, because if one thing was certain about him, he was nobody's victim. But one fact he wanted to share with me, so long as I kept it to myself, was that the Vatican had announced only a year ago, in 1974, that the Jews no longer bore collective responsibility for the crucifixion of Christ.

Sitting in non-assembly with Woody was a robustly built boy whose given name was Anil. When Mr Evans realised he had a Hindu in class he went to great trouble to look into Hinduism, and our imaginations were caught by the reverence in which Hindus held cattle. It was but a short step for Anil's broad shoulders and his religion's prize beast to combine in his new name, which he absolutely adored – Oxen.

We didn't have the foggiest about Oxen's Hinduism. He seemed exactly like us, only a bit browner. When we went back to his house, it was a surprise to find his mum in a sari and images of the elephant god Ganesh on the walls. Even more of a shock was that his entire family had started calling him Oxen.

It was easy to make a mistake about Oxen's family. At first I thought they were always in the same room together because they were poor. They were not; his father was a doctor. It was hard for me to grasp that they sat in the same room from choice; that, culturally and religiously, family was supreme. Perfect hosts to a visiting child, the only thing I could do in return was to be their son's friend without judgement or prejudice, and as a child that comes more naturally than not.

Actually, there was one other thing I had to do for Oxen: he hand-picked me for a very important task. One morning after a swimming class he came across to me as I dried off by my peg.

'I want you to look at my penis,' he said.

Quick as a flash he lowered the front of his trunks and presented me with said item. Just as quickly he put it away.

'Did you see it?'

'Er, yes.'

'Are you sure?'

'Certain.'

'Good. Now please would you go and tell all the other chaps?'

'That you've shown me your penis?'

'No. That I have got a penis.'

He went back to his peg and dressed discreetly inside his towel like a dowager on the beach at Eastbourne. As we walked back to class I asked him what he wanted me to do. I just didn't understand. He told me that part of his Hindu upbringing involved physical modesty, not showing your nakedness to anyone except your eventual wife. Some of the other boys, and I soon guessed who (a boy called Pubes was the worst of the name-callers), had taunted him for this and speculated that his shyness in the changing rooms arose from lack of a male member.

I was in an awkward spot. I had no intention of spending lunchtime telling everyone that Oxen had shown me his penis. Neither of us would have come well out of that. Yet he had opened up to me in the most trusting way and let me see inside both his trunks and his religion. I reasoned that maybe he knew I wouldn't issue a press release, but that if the subject arose in future I might come forward as witness for the defence. The subject never did, but for any contemporaries now curious, I am happy to confirm that the young man you knew as Oxen was at that time fitted with a single, standard issue Hindu penis.

Wacko

If the Church of England had anything at all going for it, and in the mid seventies it teetered on the brink of irrelevance, it was that if you'd been signed up without your consent at your christening and had drifted away, you could rejoin the fold consciously at your confirmation. Nobody twisted your arm. It was a free choice. Like everything about the C of E at that time, confirmations were hardly rock and roll, but they had the virtue of being affirmative acts akin to deliberately choosing membership of a political party rather than just following the family line.

Catholics did it differently. Rome's view was that if a child happened to die before it was christened, it fell into limbo, the legion of the undead. Not good news. Catholics got on with their christenings swiftly, and no sooner was the washing-up dried than the young primary school Catholic was making their first communion. Thereafter he or she was a fully-fledged member of the faith, the only way out being to lapse – a mortal sin.

My friend Woody had a bar mitzvah when he became a son of the covenant. During the school term leading up to it, his Jewish afro was sheared into a wavy Starsky. He looked better for it, and the success with girls made more sense. He talked about preparing for the bar mitzvah a lot, but none of his school friends got an invitation. Bar mitzvah, for Woody, was more about being kissed by aunties and pleasing his parents than fasting like a brave desert nomad, and he was damned if he was going to do that in front of his mates.

The other observances his family kept had a vitality about them we admired, drawing deep on traditions created when the Jews were wandering the Middle East. Rosh Hashanah, Jewish New

Year, came in September when the crops were in, and you could think hard about the previous year's sins for ten days. After that came Yom Kippur, the Day of Atonement, the last chance to close the book on what you wish you hadn't done.

We weren't invited to Oxen's Hindu Upanayana either, but that was less surprising. Scriptural kinship between Judaism and Christianity was well-recognised, but none of us had the first idea about Brahma or Vishnu or Shiva, or the ceremony Oxen underwent when a long white cotton thread was placed over his left shoulder and under his right arm, a strand for each of the three gods. One day in the changing rooms, Oxen changed his pants as ever under the big towel and stood before us with this triple thread modestly on view, reminding him of his debt to his god, his ancestors and his spiritual teacher. It looked like a bit of old string to us, but he used to put it in his valuables bag with his watch and his wallet, and from that point on we respected its importance.

We were even more clueless about Islam, and would remain so for some decades to come. Curiously, we went round singing a word which, if we had bothered to look it up, would have led us to understand the first Muslim rite of passage. We were inspired to do so by the extraordinary male soprano of Freddie Mercury, whose Bohemian Rhapsody contained many terms we did not know. Fandango, for example, Scaramouch, and Beelzebub. Coming in on a low bass note, the rest of Queen intoned 'Bismillah. No, we will not let you go'. In our ignorance we didn't know that a few miles away in east London, thousands of young Muslims were named in the ceremony of Aqiqah, spoke their first verses of the Koran aged four at Bismillah, and expressed their commitment as teenagers with their first fast at Ramadan.

Woody would have been the only one of us who had a chance with all that, but would he have known how close so many Islamic practices were to Judaism? Was he interested that when Mohammed met with no success converting the Jews, he changed the direction of prayer from Jerusalem to Mecca, replaced Saturday with Friday as the Sabbath, and displaced the feast of Atonement with the fast of Ramadan? No, like all of us he thought only of Freddie Mercury's hair and Brian May's guitar solo and the rumour that Freddie was something called a Zoroastrian, reputed to be fire-worshippers from ancient Persia.

In the context of all these evocative celebrations and first rites, it was astonishing that the most visually startling of all of them was what happened to Luke, an old friend from my primary school, at the church of the Bromley Baptists, considered then to be the most vanilla-flavoured faith. To become baptised was especially important for him because, like all members of his church, he hadn't been christened. Other major religions claimed ownership of a child at the earliest possible opportunity, but it was a founding principle of the Baptist Church in 1609 that a baby did not have the faculties to decide to join them. That could only be done after studying the Bible, when a young person was ready to make a knowing commitment to Jesus.

I'd been to the Baptists' a few times before and it was a friendly but uninspired place, a truer reflection of the real Bromley than other fancier places of worship. Baptists were the first non-conformists to take hold in Britain, and their determination that Jesus and not the monarch was head of their church had put them in the awkward squad for centuries. They weren't posh, but they were very socially committed, doing a lot of community youth work, running football teams, clubs, their own Scout units and so on.

They were very strong on Sunday school too. I went once with Luke, and suffered two hours of terrifying boredom in a room of children who seemed at first sight to know nothing about anything. Later I realised that the price of non-conformity is extreme conformity within church precincts, and that shooting my hand up to answer all the Bible study questions must have seemed to the meek teacher like an invasion by a feral child. That went against their grain, which was mild, courteous, class-free, seemingly lacking vision but teeth-grittingly determined to do things their way.

I was surprised, then, on the day of Luke's baptism, to discover that on this occasion they had as high a sense of theatre as any Victorian fairy production. I'd had no idea that concealed in an area of floor at the front of the pews was an enormous trap door, which when lifted hid a pool big enough to give hydrotherapy to a pony. This was very impressive to my boyish eye, but it was what happened next which left such an indelible memory.

Forty potential Baptists, mostly teenagers but some adults too, came in lines from a back room dressed in long white robes. They were summoned to the steps of the pool and approached the minister, who was already up to his waist in water. He was in white robes too, but given how long he would have to stand in this large cold bath, he had a wetsuit and waders on underneath.

The candidates walked into the pool, made their commitment, received the baptismal blessing and fell backwards until they were fully immersed. The minister and his assistant, supporting their backs, brought them upright, and the new Baptist walked up the steps at the other end to begin their life in Jesus.

The potency of this was obvious. Anyone who has closed their eyes in the bath and drifted under water or floated in the sea can empathise with the way mind and body respond to giving themselves to the water for a few moments. It can wash all your troubles away. I could see and respect that, but, despite the powerful theatricality of the ritual, I was even more affected by what came next. The newly baptised stood in rows smiling at friends and parents until all forty had been dunked. Yet was it possible I was the only one in the church wondering if it was intended to present us with a religiously inspired wet T-shirt contest? Luke might as well have worn his underpants, striped like a humbug, on the outside of his white robe, so clearly were they to be seen. But I only had eyes for a young woman called Kathy, who was smiling at me, oblivious of the fact that I could see her nipples, pubic hair and, when she walked away to get changed, her bum.

Afterwards there was a really friendly party at the back of the church – ham sandwiches, sausage rolls and, the elixir of modern Christian discourse, cups of coffee. I've always hated coffee so I felt a bit of an outsider. When Luke bounded over I felt even more alien.

'Jesus, Luke, everyone could see your pants.'

He tensed. 'You can't say that in here.'

'Pants?'

'No, Jesus. Not like you've just said it.'

'I'm sorry.' I shook my head in wonder. 'But did you see Kathy?'

'No. She's over there.'

'I don't mean now. I mean after she'd got all wet.'

'No, I didn't.'

I was bursting, screaming to tell him I'd seen her as good as naked. But I was also aware that at every single level this would grossly insult her, him, their parents, the history of their church, Jesus Christ Our Saviour, John the Baptist and God. So I didn't, and what I went away with that afternoon was some small insight into what it must have been like for the proper Jesus, the unequivocal good guy, to wrestle with Satan and somehow, by the skin of his teeth, overcome him. None of which could take away the fact that I, Paul Arnott, had seen, oh my God, Kathy from the Baptists' tits.

There would be no nudity when it eventually came to my own confirmation into the Church of England aged fourteen, but there was plenty of drama in the months before. One of the central obstacles to Anglicanism is that it is so fiendishly hard to grasp. Twenty of us, from a year-group of one hundred and fifty, chose to give up our lunchtimes for a term while the school chaplain, Holy Joe, sucked on his pipe and tried to sell us the idea of the Three in One.

Holy Joe was not an easy fellow. Like so many priests, he had a difficult son, an older boy one soon learned not to cross paths with. Holy Joe was old, bald, reeked of smoke and had quite large blue eyes. He struck me as a Christian who had not won the battle with vanity, as much an actor as a believer, speculating in our small study groups that Jesus must have had amazing eyes, all the while gazing at us with his own impressive peepers like the snake from *The Jungle Book*. Later, when we'd properly qualified and started taking communion from him, he'd come over all method actor.

'Take, eat, this is my blood which is given for you and for many,' he would whisper, eyes rolling into the back of his head. He seemed to have found another level in the Eucharist. It wasn't that he'd abandoned himself to the Catholic doctrine of transubstantiation, when bread and wine literally become the body and blood of Christ. He looked like he was actually trying to channel Jesus. We didn't really like this part of Holy Joe's shtick, and we didn't much care for the way he thought. He incarnated nothing at all of the motivations we had for getting confirmed in the first place.

The leading movements opposing tyranny in Communist eastern Europe, or racism and rank exploitation in Africa, were Christian. Christ's obvious empathy for the poor and meek and his disdain for authority still resounded with us two thousand years later. Our troubles might be pimples compared to those in Poland or South Africa, but in 1975 London you didn't have to be eccentric to think that much of our national life was falling apart and the old farts in charge were not up to fixing it. Our worries that year included nuclear obliteration, war in Cambodia, inflation, power strikes, daily murders in the north of Ireland, and weak leadership in the England soccer team and the Greater London Council. In that context, signing on for the church of the meek and mild seemed like a productive idea.

Holy Joe did all he could from within his clouds of pipe smoke to explain to us that Jesus was God made man and that he had come to Earth to suffer for all of our sins, from those of Adam and Eve to anything we might have in the pipeline. Then he indoctrinated us in the Holy Trinity, Father, Son and Holy Ghost. I can't say that any of us really understood what the hell he was on about. It was all so dry and theoretical; it made no natural sense.

What we could understand was the Sermon on the Mount, Jesus riling authority figures, that his courage was punished by a cruel death, and that he was an ideal man we felt we'd do well to emulate. He said the unsayable, he was unpolitical and courageous. But to my horror, Holy Joe didn't seem to buy into any of that. His Christianity was High Table at Oxford while ours was picnic table in the park. His Jesus was academic; ours was more of a suburban revolutionary.

I felt the need, quite deeply, to have faith that either God or Nature had made at least one decent human worthy of my praise because the authority figures overseeing our destiny then seemed so dysfunctional. That's why I took the first steps along a well-worn path – where an adolescent expresses his disaffection with society, not by spraying expletives on a railway arch but by affirming his belief in a Christian Church.

That spring term I read my Bible, was extra nice to parents and friends, and prayed quietly every night, which seemed to work. I felt as if I was approaching a significant fork in the road and coming nearer to a universal truth.

Then something bizarre and beyond any reasonable expectation took place. For the first time in decades, the headmaster of the Middle School, Mr Stephen Howard, took it upon himself to give three of the young men in his care the cane.

One of them was me.

And there was a Judas in our midst.

It was Tuesday mid-morning after first break – double Physics. The omens were bad. Yet again my electrical circuit didn't work. Across the classroom other boys were installing theirs into little windmills or motion detectors. I still couldn't tell AC from DC.

There was a knock at the door. It was a prefect sent with a message from Mr Howard. The message was for me. All eyes followed as I made my way out of the science block towards the deputy head's office. Crossing a car park in the sunshine, I thought of reasons why he might want to see me. I'd been playing in the under-14 rugby and hockey teams, was about to be confirmed, had decent enough marks, bar Physics. I couldn't quite bring it all into focus, but it occurred to me that maybe I was up for some kind of prize; not the one for achievement that was on permanent display at Michael's house, but maybe a bronze gong for effort or willingness.

Mr Howard's office hadn't been made over since about 1880: rugs, classical busts, green Wellingtons in the corner. Very untechnocratic. I walked in jauntily, unaware that I was entering a court martial.

My chrome-domed judge and jury was sitting gravely behind his oak desk with his moustache.

'Sit down. Arnott, I want you to think back to a Tuesday evening six weeks ago when you were returning from school on the train.'

I thought back. Nothing.

'I can't think of anything, sir.'

'Come on, Arnott. An incident involving thrown sandwiches in a first-class compartment.'

'Oh, that.'

'That, Arnott. The school has received a complaint from an occupant of the carriage. She says that the sandwich landed on her attaché case, and further, when she attempted to disembark at Shortlands a door was slammed in her face.'

My head was swimming. No effort prize here. What I remembered was that half a dozen of us had been going home in our tatty Army corps uniforms after staying behind for a fruitless hour parading across the playground. The train was bursting with commuters and we'd had to get into the corridor of First Class. Admittedly we'd been a little rowdy, and one boy (N) had thrown a sandwich at another (C), which he ducked. It had indeed landed on this lady's case, for which C had apologised. My entire part in this scandal was to be present at the time.

Of all of us, N was the most likely to cause trouble. A curious case, he took to sexual waters at an absurdly young age, years ahead of the rest of us, and had already been, in the biblical sense, with a girl from James Allen's Girls' School. He was a Catholic, and even more curiously was the only boy I knew who had earlier shown interest in his own sex too.

I explained the sandwich incident from the onlooker perspective to Mr Howard. A true account, it did not play well.

'The witness further claims the use of foul and abusive language,' he spluttered.

I knew what that was. When N had left the train at Shortlands he had accidentally shut the door in the face of this woman. She had said out loud 'Do you mind!', and he, presumably not realising she had already opened the window, invited her to F— off.

'That wasn't me, sir.'

'Then who was responsible?'

'I don't know, sir.'

'I think it may well have been you.'

'It wasn't.'

'What would you do now in my position, Arnott? Dulwich does not relish letters such as this. The lady concerned speaks of taking the matter to the authorities if she does not gain satisfaction from the school.'

I puffed my cheeks slightly and exhaled.

'Sir, I can see it sounds bad, but to be honest, sir, I think she might be exaggerating.'

The trap slammed.

'Your difficulty in making an assertion of that nature, Arnott, is that the lady in question is a recently retired chief inspector from New Scotland Yard. That makes her a reliable witness, in my book, and rather closer to the authorities than the school would like.'

'I'm sorry, sir.'

Oh dear, it was going to be Extra Lesson and a letter home. Bollocks. And just as I was getting ready to be confirmed, too. It was so ironic. For years I was a hooligan on those trains home, but now I behaved like an old dear myself. Guilty of many previous undetected offences, I was genuinely innocent of this one. What were the theological implications of this? Was it a cleaning of the slate, or a pre-confirmation reminder of the strange ways in which God moved? Was injustice good for the soul?

'I am left with no alternative, Arnott. There were three of you involved. E has already had two across the palm, but since I judge you and N to be the principal culprits, I will give you both the same. Three on the rump.'

Jesus Christ, he was going for a cane. As far as I was aware, nobody had been caned since the war. I couldn't believe he even had one on school premises. I suspected it was against the law.

'Lean across that chair, Arnott.'

I did as I was told.

'This will hurt me more than it hurts you,' he said, preparing to strike, presumably retrieving a memory of what he'd been told when he was at school with Tom Brown. This was untrue. The pain was nothing. It was the betrayal that hurt.

'That is the end of the matter, Arnott. You may return to your class.'

I left his study to be confronted with the familiarly self-satisfied N waiting outside. I wondered what the effect would be of tipping him off about what was coming his way, but decided that since it was his F— off and his sandwich which had caused this scrape, he could fend for himself. He had always seemed expert at playing the big man.

The sun was still shining as I walked back to the remainder of double Physics. Mr Tumber, one of a sub-set of young teachers with post-hippy beards, had either gone to fetch some stationery or to have a swift smoke, so when on my return ten friends asked what Stevie H had wanted, we were free to talk.

'You're not going to believe this,' I said, hardly doing so still myself, 'but he's just caned me.'

'Yeah, crap.'

The disbelief was total. I would have reacted in the same way. It was an anachronism, about as likely as Mr Howard taking me for a ride on a penny-farthing. I turned round, unzipped my trousers, lowered my underpants and treated the class to my smarting buttocks. It occurs to me now that this must have hurt them more than it hurt me. Their parents could not have expected, over the cornflakes, that their sons would spend one half of the morning on circuit boards and the other looking at three fresh welts on a fellow's bum.

That lunchtime the word spread faster than wildfire, and with it a chain of events began to fall into place. N, predictably, bigged himself up with regard to both the original incident and the badge of honour on his rear. C had played no part. E, the one who had taken two across the hand – which sounded much more painful than our rump shots – had been the first suspect. He had clearly done nothing to protect either me or N and had indeed put us both firmly in the frame. (He's a solicitor now.)

The question was, how Mr Howard had got to E. And that is where one other character must be introduced – L.

The trail of evidence had begun with him. The beady-eyed ex-chief inspector had seen L's name on his school bag and cited him in her letter of complaint. L was summoned by Mr Howard and had sung like a canary. This revelation took all the wind from my sails, for, of all things, L was the head of the Junior Christian Union, a Jesus freak. My understanding of the Christian spirit was that you'd rather be crucified than give up one of your own. I saw no excuse in his only being sixteen. It seemed so gutless, and for a while I wondered if I wanted to be confirmed into the same outfit as him after all.

I just couldn't get this thought from the front of my mind, and after a few days I simply had to discuss it with him face to face. We sat in a hidden corner of the library where he was brave enough to weep with shame in front of another boy. Forgiveness and understanding came as a reflex, and I was instantly back on the righteous path. Maybe there was something in this Christian ethos after all. Perhaps they only said 'I'm Spartacus' in the movies.

That evening my parents were outraged, impressively so. They'd had cause before to be concerned about moderate bad behaviour on my part, but with my confirmation looming, and the daily straightening of my act plain to see, they took my part entirely. The next morning they drove directly to school with me fretting in the back of the car and demanded to see Mr Howard immediately. This was unprecedented conduct on their part; usually they backed any figure of authority to the hilt.

We were back in the same corridor. I sat outside as my father led the way in. I heard less than gruntled tones, and five minutes later they were seen out by Mr Howard, his red cheeks burning.

'Goodbye, dear,' Betty said to me. 'We'll see you later.' She had the great good sense not to kiss me. Peter gave me an affirmative nod and they left.

'Arnott, would you come in for a moment, please.'

He would have asked me to sit down but probably feared I couldn't.

'You may have guessed that your parents did not approve of my action yesterday, but I have reassured them that the reason I acted as such was so as to close the wound with no more further ado. Your father has asked me to point out to you that therefore this will not appear on your school record.'

A few days after he'd whacked me with the cane, the stripe effect was gone. As I prepared for my confirmation, the incident somehow added yeast to the mix. I thought harder about the Christian morality of whether it was right that I be punished when I was innocent when I'd so often eluded justice when guilty. I thought harder about the issue of turning the other cheek, no pun intended. All I could do was forgive. So I did. As is now clear, I did not forget.

A few weeks later I was confirmed by the Bishop of Southwark, the future social campaigning Bishop of Liverpool and ex-cricketer David Sheppard. We would have wondered if he washed his socks by night but he was too heroic a figure for this. As ever, we had to fight our way to the finishing line through stifled laughter. A guest preacher presented a series of deliberately false assertions about Christianity and then declaimed, 'I say Rhubarb, Rubbish to that'. Why had nobody told him this was not a great oratorical device from a man unable to pronounce his r's?

Back at home Betty threw a tea party for her friends, and I could feel her pride. One of them, a Catholic from an Irish background, gave me a monstrous crucifix with a body of Christ hanging from it, the like of which would not be seen again until Mel Gibson's lunatic *The Passion of the Christ*. For many years I had to make sure it was on a nail above my bed when her family came round but if I'd ever had any leanings towards Rome, that horrible object would have cured me.

Greece is the Word

My act was now clean and I was a fledgling member of the Church of England. On Tuesday mornings before school I attended Holy Communion with fifty other lesser spotted Christians. When the chaplain rolled his eyes into his head and groaned, 'We are not worthy so much as to gather up the crumbs under thy table,' I no longer sniggered.

Before, during and after communion, I prayed. At home, on my own in a cold room with a single bed, a monkish cell, I prayed too. In an earlier time these might have been the first footsteps to becoming a rosy-cheeked country parson. In the brutish London of the 1970s the stigma in even considering this out loud was potent.

My friendship with the atheist future astronomer, Michael, had gone cold over the years. He was a good cricketer, and this seemed to be his only contact with the mainstream boys as he slogged his way towards an unfeasible stack of A-grade O levels and became one of a tiny inner sanctum allowed to programme the science-fiction phenomenon we mortals had heard of but were destined never to see, 'the computer'.

I could sense a problem – that we feeble-minded arts side boys were encouraged to deal in maybes while the scientists were shown the royal road to certainty. This did not seem wholly deserved, for a lot of the things presented to us as scientific fact felt wrong. We spent one long afternoon on the theory of evolution, which was, of course, exciting and made the little grey cells dance. The response in my imagination was that Man himself must still be evolving, and I gave voice to this, only to be told by the Biology teacher in very certain terms that Man was essentially the finished article. This made no sense to me. We'd only been around for a couple of hundred thousand years and came in all shades and sizes adapted for different environments and means of survival. Weren't we one of the very best examples of continuing evolution? I was sure he must be wrong about this, but the biology teacher's faith in the rightness of science was beyond challenge, which made me wonder if this wasn't as much a field of convictions and hunches, albeit tested by experimentation, as making a sculpture.

In most scientific endeavour I was as good as drowned. It seems lazy to make excuses about the uselessness of the teaching, though you had to be there to believe it, and so the answer was to blame oneself for not being at ease dealing with the abstract. Because I couldn't see or touch radio waves or atoms, the theories I was meant to understand left no useful imprint in my mind. Yet when it came to the written word and to language, I'd conjure with the abstract as happily as watch *Match of the Day*.

For every new step Michael took into abstract scientific thinking, he was given positive reinforcement in praise and exam results, whereas my form of abstract exploration in matters of religion on repeated solo flights through the Bible was not reinforced at all. If I had mentioned it to a soul it would have been judged eccentric. There was no forum for it. Compulsory curriculum RE had ended to allow for more sterile hours with the Bunsen burner.

This was disappointing, because I felt I'd discovered something when reading the Bible on hot evenings with Kate Bush warbling in the background that had never been revealed, like discovering a Dead Sea Scroll – that, according to which of the four Gospels one read, the final words of Jesus on the cross had a blindingly different significance.

In John's gospel, Jesus says he is thirsty and a sponge soaked in vinegar is cruelly pushed into his mouth. He knows he is about to die, and with that he will fulfil the scriptures. Then, death comes:

'He said, "it is finished": and he bowed his head and gave up the ghost.'

In both Matthew and Mark's accounts he seems to feel not that he has just finished playing a prophesied part, but that he has been betrayed by God:

'*Eli, Eli, lema sabachthani*? Which means My God, My God, why hast thou forsaken me?'

This is shocking, the son of God questioning his father's cruelty with his dying breath; they are the last words of a man not at all reconciled to its ending like this.

Yet the nuance in Luke is different again:

'Father, into thy hands I commend my spirit: and having said thus, he gave up the ghost.'

It was as if a great novelist wasn't sure how to finish his story. Would it be a brave and resigned ending, with the lifting of a great burden at the end of an epic tale, like John's version? Would it be the self-pity of Matthew and Mark's account, with its depressive undercurrent of Tony Hancock's 'Stone me, what a life'? Or was it to be Luke's sense of peace from the faith that he'd meet his father in the next world? It seemed to me, as I ate my packed lunch, that both death and Christianity had three natures: resigned, or despairing, or filled with new hope. These were profoundly different readings of life's purpose and the significance of death. Never mind the Periodic Table, these were the big questions.

There were other Christians about the place, of course, but unlike me they seemed to be already house-trained, reluctant to ask awkward questions. The tart campness of the pair of boys considered most likely to be heading for ordination was generally tolerated, though they were not an especially affirmative advertisement for the meek. Their proclaimed 'faith' was scoffed at by the barbaric horde, especially when one of them had the misfortune to twist his testicles in an inter-form rugby match. Never had the gentle whisper from Mary, the school nurse – 'I'm afraid this might hurt a bit' – been more apposite as she untweaked his gonads in the medical room. His howl was heard across the school grounds, and the atheistic throng mocked that if that was how Jesus looked after his own, the unfortunate twistee could keep it.

This did not amuse me. I was becoming a young man who really tried to do good, and why not? When an aggressive boy, an international fencing competitor, placed a rubbish bin over the classroom door so as to bring it down on the head of a bumbling English teacher, I dismantled his trap. This was a mere gesture compared with Claus von Stauffenberg taking on the Führer in the Wolf's Lair, but one small blow against tyranny for me in the Fourth Form.

I had already marked the Fencer's card. He should have lost sleep later in life for his treatment during our O level English talks of an overweight boy known unkindly as Whaley. Whaley's talk was a charming but vulnerable lecture on his passion for the vintage radio comedy, *The Goon Show*, enlivened by his own impressions of Neddie Seagoon, Bluebottle, and Eccles. It wasn't going to get a night at the London Palladium, but it was an enthusiastic effort. We all chuckled supportively, except for the gimlet-eyed Fencer.

A few days later it was the turn of the Fencer to give his talk. We had been encouraged by the English teacher to keep our topics as a surprise for the rest of the form. This could backfire. One well-mannered lad announced, 'Today I am going to speak to you about Chinese Snuff Boxes' and was greeted with such laughter I imagine he never spoke of them again.

When the Fencer rose to his feet, he simply said, 'Yeah, well, I got the idea for this talk the other day. It's about the relationship between obesity and a complete lack of a sense of humour.'

What could have made him think we would enjoy the next ten minutes of cruelty at Whaley's expense? Certainly he was in-genious, talking knowledgeably about varying degrees of obesity and genres of radio comedy. Then he ruthlessly honed in on his diabolical synthesis – that the low esteem of a fat boy could be boosted by lousy attempts at impersonating other people's comic inventions. Whaley sat scarlet with embarrassment, trying not to sob out loud in his seat in the back row.

That's why I didn't let the Fencer hurt the English teacher. I was bigger than him, but the reflexes acquired in his sport would probably have landed me in deep trouble if we'd fought. I can't say he respected me for resisting him; I think he just thought I was a tosser. I wasn't. I was a young Christian trying to do the right thing.

In the months after my confirmation I'd seemed to find a level balance in prayer. I didn't hear any voice of God in reply to my questions, but then my questions were rhetorical. I did find layer after layer of new insight and reassurance as the habit became longer-standing, a well of resolve I could draw on in conflicts such as this. And then the school decided to take a party of boys to Greece. My parents kindly cobbled together the fare in exchange for a year of car cleaning. I wouldn't say they were fussy customers, but I'd use my last £3 on programme one at the car wash rather than suffer the chapped hands and chamois leathers of that winter of discontent.

My knowledge of Greece, ancient or modern, was lamentable. In my last year at primary school we'd been taken to the New Theatre in Bromley to see a puppet production of *The Odyssey*. I was so enthralled, especially by Odysseus hiding from Cyclops clinging to the underside of a sheep, and by his resisting the lure of the Sirens by tying himself to a mast, ears stuffed with beeswax, that it might have seeded a potential classicist, but the trip was superseded by the drama of an event which happened later in the week.

A Christian superstar was due to appear in a play at the struggling New Theatre. Cliff Richard. The ladies of Bromley were beside themselves. Betty and all her coffee-morning chums had tickets hidden in their biscuit barrels, but they woke on the morning of the first show to the news that the theatre had burned to the ground. Somehow, every time a Greek myth was mentioned after that I thought of Cliff, and now that I've had years to bone up on the subject I wonder if there wasn't a real connection after all in the story of Narcissus.

There wasn't much of the Ancient World to be sensed in daily life in Dulwich, but on arrival in Athens there seemed to be little else. It was viscerally ancient, pungent with difference and surprise. On the pavement opposite our shabby hotel, a group of prostitutes hung out all day, smoking with their legs wide open. You didn't see this in Tenby. For dinner on our first night we were served stewed goat. On our first walk around Constitution Square as a rabble of youths without our teachers, we encountered soldiers in lace skirts and pom-poms on their shoes. We ate our first ever pistachio nuts and we smelled lemon juice squirted over pavement kebabs.

Back at the hotel we failed, at first, to engage with any aspect of modern Greece. A puff of nationalistic pride billowed around us when we saw that the Greeks were devoted to English football on TV, cheering as Gordon Hill scored two wonder-goals for Manchester United in the F.A. Cup. When they cut back to one of their own matches, the waiters all cleared off to the kitchen.

The next night we gathered round the telly again and watched our nation trounce all comers in the European Song Contest with Brotherhood of Man's 'Save Your Kisses for Me'. Even though none of us could stand the hand-jiving, flared-trousered old tat, we'd still won, and it was better than the Nana Mouskouri inflicted on us during *The Val Doonican Show* back home. We bellowed our victory song across the street, now deserted by the prostitutes who were hard at it in the flats above. We shamed the memory of our forebears, delicate Hellenists such as Lord Byron, who got all worked up over a Grecian Urn, though perhaps there was something Spartan in the devotion of so many of us to pig-ignorance about our new surroundings.

Yet into our uncouth youth the many ages of the Ancient Greeks began to seep. The Mycenaean, the Doric, Ionic, Archaic,

Hellenic. This did not come from the string of on-site lectures we were treated to by our adorable old teacher Mr 'Pop' Palmer, the depth of whose knowledge was matched only by his inability to communicate any of it as the sun grilled our bored young heads and he shuffled sheaves of A4 in his hands. If we wanted to leave a site any the wiser, the few of us who were interested had to gather pamphlets and read explanatory plaques.

Infinitely richer as a source of knowledge was Irini, our guide. Her style was electrifying by contrast with Pop Palmer. Every morning she appeared on the steps of our coach wearing hues of black, brown and grey, her dark hair streaked with blond dye, her fingers and toes multi-ringed. We anticipated her arrival with open mouths and she never disappointed. It did not seem possible, but as one day rolled into the next she found another centimetre to trim from the bustline of her dress, until one evening at dinner her breasts seemed to sit on the table between us.

While Pop gave us the daily benefit of half a century's learning from atop an ancient slab of marble, we would shuffle closer to Irini. To win her attention we asked devious strings of questions about her country and its gods. I loved language and was thrilled to hear her explain the words her ancestors had given to mine. Ostracism, strategy, hysteria, grammar, politics, gymnasium, logic, apathy. Gynaecology. Religion.

It was for Irini that I showed off at Olympia, as only a fourteen and a half year old boy can, repeatedly sprinting the hundred or so metres of the arena where the first games were held. At Cape Sounion at sunset, I posed with my shirt off, leaning against either a Doric or an Ionic column (never was clear about that), hoping that she'd see me twitching my pecs. And in the amphitheatre at Epidaurus I sat close to her as she told me that orchestra was a Greek word too. Then she asked me how old I was and I pretended not to hear.

One night we were staying away from Athens, near Mycenae, and she danced with us at a disco to 'That's the Way (I Like It)' by KC and the Sunshine Band, each hoping it was us she was really dancing with. Even as we danced I hoped she didn't feel intimidated, that she didn't feel she was surrounded by a clutch of frenzied satyrs. What was wrong with me? I hadn't yet read John Fowles' *The Magus*, but I was behaving like one of its characters – the restrained young Christian Englishman who loses his marbles and his self-control in the first flash of Mediterranean sun.

After a long coach journey ascending winding roads to Delphi, Irini set me straight. We were there to see the home of the Oracle, and Pop was destroying our will to live, again, with a tortoise-paced lecture on the Pythia, the priestess who communicated the words of Apollo to the leading figures in Greek society, advising whether it was a good year for the roses or for sacking Jerusalem.

My shoulders were sagging when, just behind me, I heard Irini whisper, 'Interesting, huh?'

I turned. She was smiling complicitly and walked away down the steps of a temple and towards a waterfall. She scooped up some water and splashed her face. I went to do the same.

'Don't drink. Only wash.'

We could look down on the school party now and we carried on along a path until I began to wonder where she was leading me. Then she sat down on a rock and took me aback.

'You are a Christian, yes?'

I assented.

'The other boys are not, right? The one with the hair is a Jew. I asked Mr Palmer about this last night.' She smiled. 'I am a Christian too. What I am going to tell you is just for you, yes?'

I agreed readily. Where was this leading?

'I have to tell you, none what Mr Palmer speaks of interests Greeks. The ancient gods before Jesus, they all were dug up by the British. See the Oracle down there, it was covered in mud until a hundred years ago. He is telling you the wrong things about Greece.'

I asked her what she meant, realising that what she'd seen in me was not the rippling torso of an adolescent but a fellow Christian.

She transfigured before my eyes. I felt ashamed that I'd been seeing her as a pair of breasts in sunglasses.

'I spoke to Mr Palmer about this last night,' she said. 'He wants to tell you what the classicists teach in England. But because he is not a Christian he is not telling you what is the most important thing. You must know about it. I know you don't.'

I was intrigued, and, with my lust cast down into the valley below, I was captivated by what she had to say.

'I lived with my brother in New Southgate for two years. Nicholas took me to a church in Barnet. It was so dull.'

She looked meaningfully down towards the slumped figures around Pop.

'Nicholas says all English churches are the same. You have a church in Dulwich?'

'St Barnabas.'

'Barnabas made the first church in Cyprus. With Paul. And they buried Lazarus there. In Larnaca.'

I hadn't the foggiest what she was talking about. I'd been to a few parties in the church hall at St Barnabas but had never imagined that its namesake had lived or worked with Paul, the greatest evangelist of all, on Greek soil. Besides, Irini was mistaken in one of her facts.

'I don't think it can have been Lazarus,' I said. 'He was the one Jesus raised from the dead. He lived in a place called Bethany in Israel.'

Never correct a tour guide. Irini came closer and looked up into my face.

'So what do you think happened to Lazarus? Did he just stay there? He was a living miracle. All the Romans and the Jews wanted him dead. He had to flee. He ran away to Cyprus.'

'Oh. I didn't know that.'

I really didn't know that. Somewhere along the way I'd heard the legend that Pontius Pilate, who'd washed his hands over what to do with Jesus, had gone back to Rome and been convicted of some offence. He'd been taken miles by horse and cart into the

Sibillini Mountains, home to the Sibylls, the ancient cave-dwelling necromancers, and drowned in Pilate's Lake, named, presumably, after rather than before the event. Yet I hadn't considered that bit-part players like Lazarus had had an off-stage afterlife too. I could feel how featherweight my Christian history was. In England you only seemed to be told things on a need-to-know basis.

'That's why I wanted Mr Palmer to let me talk to you all about something, but he won't let me. He said this is not a Christian trip.'

'What did you want to say?'

'That all the churches in England are dead. And you come here to find out about gods we don't even believe in and you ignore the most important fact that is staring at you in the face.'

'What?'

'You believe in God?'

'Well, sort of. It's hard to explain. But at a basic level—'

'Of course, you are confused. Like the church in Barnet. But God is here. In Greece. It is where the word of Jesus first came. It has been the same ever since. We have not changed. Your churches try to understand things you never can. Like the Holy Trinity.'

I thought back to Holy Joe's meanderings on that topic, as opaque as Pop's theories on Greek weaponry.

'Well, none of us really have a clue what to make of all that,' I said.

'This is because you've spent centuries separating them, trying to find who is the most important, the Father, the Son, the Holy Spirit. None of them are. They are one. They always have been. That is what we know here in Greece. There are things called paradoxes. You cannot know the answers to them all. You must live with them. And you must love the life of Christ.'

She was magnificent. She had seen through the vanity of a teenage boy and realised that somewhere inside was a mind looking for answers. Just as I couldn't allow the Fencer to hurt the English teacher, so she couldn't allow me to return to London with the wrong epistle from her country.

She was full of surprises. That day was her last as our guide and without ceremony she left us. We never saw her again, and I couldn't discuss with any of my friends what she had told me. I was a quiet Christian if I was one at all, and I didn't want to be exiled from the lads' camp; and in any case the chances of my reaching the end of a sentence opening with a meditation on the Orthodox Church were nil.

I stopped noticing the prostitutes across the road and began to notice the bearded priests shopping in the flea market, paying from shiny leather purses under layers of cloth. Pop never took us into a church. We never saw any icons. I didn't learn that such paintings were venerated in Greek Orthodoxy for their own holiness, for their literal depiction of the goodness of Christ. That they were regarded as an aperture through which divinity could be seen. We did not learn about the iconoclasts, the whitewashers of divinely inspired churches, nor did we have the opportunity to compare them with our own Puritans who sacked English churches centuries later, removing nearly all traces of the vivid paintings which had graced the walls and ceilings, obliterating them at the behest of goons rampant from the days of Elizabeth I to Oliver Cromwell. We could not connect the Greek Church to the eventual blossoming of its cousin, the Russian Orthodox, via Bulgaria; nor did we see that at the very time we were in Greece, just after the government of the Generals, it was that same repressed Orthodox Church in Russia that was the main focus of opposition and hope. I can make those connections now, and I am grateful for this to Irini and her oracle at Delphi for this. But for want of the intellectual resources to develop her ideas at that early point in my spiritual journey, our Greek trip relapsed to the level of earthier matters.

Pop Palmer carried on as before. Jesus wept. Any sight of the sea sparked ramblings about the Third War of the Peloponnesians and the naval cunning of the Persians. We wanted to scream out loud that we didn't care. We were there for a suntan and a good time with our friends.

And so our minds turned to mischief. Our journey to Athens had begun at Luton Airport, ranked for international glamour, at the time, somewhere between Woolworth's and Butlin's. We had hung around as coolly as we knew how and drawn the gazes of the girls of the Strathaven Academy from Lanarkshire in Scotland. One lassie had checked out our luggage labels and figured that our destinies were triply intertwined. We were all flying Monarch Airways. We were landing in Athens. And we were all staying at the Hotel Apollo.

Relations were opened, and as our slightly depressurised Monarch biplane struggled over the Alps, we became aware that anonymous notes were being passed forward for our attention, bearing phrases such as 'I fancy you' and 'I French kiss'. It was like a packet of Love Hearts being handed round on the bus, only these girls had real intent.

We had just begun *Pride and Prejudice* at school, but this lot were a different species from the dainties of Jane Austen. Archive footage of 'Top of the Pops' circa 1976 will help identify the genus. We boys would have been wearing last year's clothes and bad haircuts. The girls of Strathaven would have been dancing in front of the cameras, some of their clothes lined with Tartan, like the Bay City Rollers, and their well-shampooed heads bonny with centre partings curled at the sides by hot tongs, tank tops hugging their figures, and stacked heels hiding beneath furlongs of bell-bottom.

At the hotel the notes continued. I was truly amazed, in this ancient city with balalaika music piping from cafés and chants radiating through church windows, that one of the authors had focused on me. When my friends went out for an evening to kick their heels in Athens, the two of us hid away in an empty bedroom and ravished each other in an exploratory but considerate way. By the yardstick of Lanarkshire, I behaved like Mr Darcy, leaving us both intact as our friends drifted back to the hotel. We joined them and I imagine she boasted of the experience as much as me. The night, however, was young.

The indelicate N of the caning earlier in the year had been out of luck with these willing girls. N was not satisfied by this. Realising that I had breached their defences, he insisted that I take him to the hotel room which four of the girls were sharing.

Down in the lobby, the word was out. There had been near-sex in the hotel and both schools danced with excitement. It must have been a matter of moments before this reached the ear of the Scottish headmistress. This was not the news from Marathon she had wanted to hear, and she immediately communicated her concern to Pop Palmer, who was just sitting down with a retsina on the terrace.

Meanwhile, N was trying to impress one or more of the Scottish girls. I felt odd, because the girl I had been with a few minutes before did not sleep in that room and it seemed an impropriety for me to be there. N persuaded one girl to sit next to him on the end of a bed while the rest of us chatted nervously. Before his hands could wander far, there was a brisk rap on the locked door.

'Excuse me, girls,' came the reluctant voice of Pop Palmer. 'I believe you may have one or more pupils from Dulwich College in your room. I would ask that they come out immediately.'

This presented no problem for me. N, however, had the mind of a scriptwriter for a *Carry On* film.

'Let's go,' I said.

'No, sod Pop. Let's hide.'

I followed him wearily into the bathroom, where even a man of his wits realised we'd not stay undetected long behind the shower curtain. We went back into the bedroom.

'What'll we do?' said a girl called Nancy.

'Arnott, over here.'

N had discovered a door leading on to a small balcony. I followed him outside as he made incomprehensible hand gestures to the worried girls.

'Girls,' came the off-stage voice of Mr Palmer once more. 'I wonder if you might be so kind as to—'

He was cut off by the voice of the headmistress.

'Girls, you will unlock this door right now.'

I was crouching on the balcony, and could hear what was going on through a window. N was watching it for himself through the net curtains.

'You should look at this. Old Pops is looking for us in the bathroom. What a laugh.'

'Thank you, Mr Palmer,' said the headmistress. 'I will take it from here.'

Pop plodded out of the room, apologising for having disturbed the peace. When he'd gone, the headmistress gave her verdict.

'I do not know precisely what has been going on in this room, but I am perfectly certain that you had those boys in here.'

N snorted, though even he could not have imagined what was said next.

'Now then, girls, you are to get undressed and get into bed immediately. And I am not going to leave this room until you have done so.'

'Bloody Nora,' said the poet. 'They're taking all their clothes off.'

I looked out into the Athenian night. This was wrong. 'We ought not to look.'

'Are you joking? Jesus Christ. You should see the nipples on my one.'

The scene played out for a minute. I had the radio version, with hot-breathed commentary from N. He, as ever, was taking the occasion as far as it could be pushed.

'That one's got a red bush.'

'Shut up. The teacher will hear you.'

Soon enough it was over and the headmistress was gone. N came in from the balcony, leering. I walked between the row of beds towards the door like a junior doctor on a women's ward, all discretion and respect for the privacy of womankind.

'What you doing?' said N.

'We ought to go.'

The girls nodded. N didn't say that he'd seen all he wanted anyway, but his crass face said it for him. I was ashamed.

It might appear that I had the moral upper-hand over the oafish N on that Greek trip, but I was not finished yet. The next morning I went down to breakfast, sat at a table with my white rolls and jam, looked up, and fell instantly in love with a girl called Elaine. This was awful. I bolted my breakfast, and before the rest of her friends arrived in the dining room, including my companion of the night before, I asked her to walk down the road with me to a small dusty park. There, on a swing, I declared my feelings.

'What are you saying?' she said. 'You were with Sheila last night.'

'Yeah, I know. I just think you're fantastic.'

I felt like Romeo swearing off Rosalind for Juliet in a beat. I didn't know what to do with myself. My newly joined faith could do nothing to help me. Where in either the Old or New Testament was there advice for a situation such as this? There was probably something in the stories of the Greek gods Pop Palmer had been on about for the last week, but I hadn't listened to a single syllable and I couldn't really go back to the hotel and ask him.

Then it got even worse. Word was out that I had been seen disappearing from the hotel with Elaine, and Sheila came to find us with my best friend in tow. It was a non-verbal encounter. The four of us sat on two see-saws, Elaine and I on one and the jilted Sheila with my friend on the other. Elaine was bemused, Sheila felt rejected, my friend was rightly embarrassed to be party to such a scene, and I fell deeper in with every moment.

As we walked back to the hotel, Sheila asked me what the hell I was playing at. Had last night meant nothing? I said I didn't know what she meant, and she held me back on the street as I watched Elaine heading inside.

'I really hate Elaine,' she said. 'I used to think she was dead nice.'

She was dead nice. Oh God.

The next two days were torture. I couldn't get a moment alone with Elaine, while Sheila behaved with dignified confusion. To the Tartan Army I appeared to be exactly what I was – an English bastard.

Too soon we were on separate coaches to the airport. On the plane I tried to get back to where Elaine was, but there was a wall of Sheila's friends preventing it. At Luton I still couldn't separate her from the gang. And as her coach disappeared for the long journey back up the M1 to Scotland, my heart broke. Each mile back to London was more painful than the last as the distance between us grew.

Ten years later, working in Glasgow for a few days, I tried frantically to find her in the phone book in my hotel looking over the Clyde and the demolished tenements of the Gorbals beyond, but with the idea of the Internet still dozing in California, I failed. I thought back to my trinity of young women on that wonderful trip to the Ancient World, with its gods, and God, and arid slopes dotted with olive trees, and I knew that what Irini had said was true. Some paradoxes can never be resolved.

Remains of a King

My mother's family tree was enormous. Poppa, my grandfather, had a dozen brothers and sisters. Some still lived in Bermondsey, but most had escaped to the south London suburbs. Poppa, the oldest, was a gentle man with great vision who opened *Kingsons*, the first postwar chain of shops south of the Thames selling radiograms and televisions. When I was very small I visited his branches in Beckenham or Penge and watched teenagers listening to 'Good Vibrations' in a corked sound booth. It seemed very glamorous.

Poppa sold out his share and retired early, moving to the house where we lived after he died. He would have been appalled to know that his death was the occasion when I first learnt a visceral fear of the unknown; that this was when I felt the terror from which so much in religion is inspired. I was terribly spooked by knowing the exact spot by a radiator in the hall where he had died from a heart attack. I used to leap across it from the bottom stair, and when waving off guests I'd never hang around there.

It's too easy for adults to forget how much they feared as children. If I wasn't scared in my own hallway, I was terrified in the woods running at the back of our road, which you could only access through an overgrown path infested year-round by a cloud of disgusting gnats. When I took our dog for a walk I sprinted through this cloud with my eyes nearly closed. When we reached the woods themselves we kept running. I could hardly travel an inch without encountering a scary corner, dangerous undergrowth in the rhododendrons, a dark lake, or a sudden opening into a gloomy glade where I felt as if hidden eyes were on me. They often were, as the trees hid woodsmen who worked for the owner. It was a matter of contention whether we were really allowed to walk freely here, and I was regularly confronted by a pair of these frightening old gits asking me what I was doing. To avoid all these things I ran and ran as a pagan might run from dark spirits.

Fear is not to be underestimated as a precursor to faith, and the world painted for us by adults at this time was filled with many terrors. There were grave ones like the threat of a post-nuclear apocalypse, middling terrors like *The Pilgrim's Progress*, broadcast at teatime on a Sunday with its skeletal depiction of death, and lighter examples such as *Dr Who*. Scariest of all was the darkness you could still feel from the horrors of war. It had ended three decades before, but there were still bomb-site car parks in towns and craters in our woods overlooking Biggin Hill airport. The police station still tested its air-raid siren every now and then. A child could feel its shadow; many books and comics were suffused with it; and words such as *Vaterland* and *Deutschland* were part of the language of evil.

I was aware of this context when, in the summer of 1977, a man called Stan said that he'd like me to help him on his next export trip to Germany. Stan was located on a remote branch of my mother's huge familial network, if only by marriage, and had given up his work as a garage mechanic to run his own business exporting British Leyland motor parts to Germany. Why any German given a free choice between an Audi and a Morris Marina would choose the latter was a mystery, but they soon learned, when bits started to fall off the Marina, that no spare parts were to be found south of the Channel.

Step forward Stan, who would fill every inch of his van with fan-belts and gear boxes until his axles groaned, and drive them to that exotic and evocative place, the Continent. He was every inch the entrepreneur, from his tinted glasses to his grey shoes. He smoked cigars, bought me my first Pils lager, kept a rude magazine in his briefcase, and clearly had a creative touch with the invoices. With my neck slightly bent under an exhaust pipe which extended into the front cab, we retraced the route across

France and Belgium of invading British troops thirty years before. We crossed into Germany at Aachen and drove through the rebuilt and industrial smoke-stack of the Ruhr. No trip to Florence or the Himalayas could have caught my imagination more. Here I was, a fifteen-year-old boy helping unload motor parts at German garages, chipping in with my O level vocabulary, allowed at last to see into the belly of the creature which had nearly destroyed us.

Our ultimate destination was Cologne. British bombs had wrought terrible destruction there, but mercifully had not entirely destroyed its astonishing black Gothic cathedral, for many years the tallest building in the world. With our final delivery made, Stan settled down outside a bar overlooking the cathedral square, and, feeling woozy on two Pils, I suggested we venture inside to have a look.

'Nah, you go on,' he said, flicking at the bottom of his Slim Panatella box and reaching for his lighter.

As he watched over me through his brown specs, topping up his tan, I walked across the square and into the strangest building I had ever seen; strange, not for its architecture, which was impressively high and wide and mighty, but for what was in it. I had come to Germany with the preconception that, as the home of Martin Luther and his Protestant reforms, its cathedrals would be high-minded and stern. In truth, that seemed to go with the stereotype of the national character too. I did not expect to find a deeply Catholic church in which I encountered holy relics for the first time. We didn't do relics in England. These weren't merely the teeth of some old saint, either. The huge golden sarcophagus in pride of place, known as the Shrine of the Three Kings, did not contain bits of former Hun or Prussian rulers. These bones had belonged to those bringers of gold, frankincense and myrrh, the three kings who had followed the star to see the baby Jesus and ridden into the sunset so as not to divulge his whereabouts to the evil Herod. A queue of Hausfrauen waited patiently to light candles before this box of old bones, and I watched them in innocent wonder, wondering how they could be so gullible.

On the way out of the building I passed the peculiarly located set of blacksmith's tongs near the doorway. These were the very implements drawn from a blacksmith's forge and still hot when applied to the extremities of a reformist who'd been allowed to preach from the pulpit by the reforming Archbishop Gebhard Truchsess von Waldburg in 1582. These hot tongs dragged the reformist out of the cathedral and earned the local blacksmiths' guild the right to bear arms within its precincts in perpetuity. The Archbishop escaped the tongs but was sacked by the Pope without delay.

Stan was still sitting outside behind enough empty bottles to run a hoopla stall. I wandered across to the bar humming 'We Three Kings' and I told him what I had discovered.

'Full of surprises these square-heads,' he said. 'Fancy another?'

Relics and indulgences make Professor Richard Dawkins' DNA boil. Of course, paying money to a church for the indulgence of being let off a few years in purgatory, or making a market in the shin-bones of saints, is not an ideal enterprise in our post-Enlightenment world. The difficulty with the Professor's disdain is that at the time of their high-water mark in the sixteenth century, his own science was full of oddities too. His forefathers hoped to turn base metal into gold, kept arsenic and mercury in the medicine chest. It looks mad now, but it made sense then.

The Church made many attempts to stop all this stuff and nonsense back then. In 1287, Bishop Quivil of Exeter demanded that a papal order against venerating relics be obeyed. 'We command the above prohibition to be carefully observed by all and decree that no person shall expose relics for sale, and that neither stones, nor fountains, trees, wood, or garments shall in any way be venerated on account of dreams or on fictitious grounds.' There were dozens of such decrees, but it was all too much fun and far too lucrative. Ironically, it forced the next stage of evolution in the Church. The overambition of another German Archbishop, Albert of Mainz, caused a crisis. In 1514, twenty-four years old, he was an archbishop in two dioceses and bishop in another, which was itself prohibited, but Pope Leo X agreed to turn a blind eye if Albert made a huge donation to Rome. To do this Albert raised a loan at the Fuggers Bank, and paid it off selling relics and indulgences.

In doing this he was only emulating his Emperor, Frederick the Wise, who collected relics with an eye on their sale value. From his catalogue you could buy a crumb from the Last Supper, a twig from the Burning Bush and a thorn from the Crown of Thorns, or for the little ones you could buy one of two hundred portions of children massacred by Herod.

Many Christians were outraged by this. When Martin Luther nailed his list of ninety-five propositions on to the door of the castle church at Wittenberg on the eve of All Saints' Day in 1517, his cause was greatly aided by the widespread despair at such ungodly doings. The Catholic Church today is clear where it stands on the authenticity of relics, admitting that most claims to possess the toenail of St Peter are so hard to be sure of that there must be some doubt. They stop short, however, of emptying the shrines on to a bonfire.

My view is that you either understand why they tolerate this obvious falsehood or you don't, on the same continuam as the fairies and Father Christmas. Scientists are allowed to look at the pickled brains of great inventors and the twisted spine of the Elephant Man when the only purpose in this must be as a kind of macabre aide-memoire; yet one wouldn't want to see all the specimen bottles smashed on the steps of the Royal Society. As someone raised in an Anglican tradition, I think relics are nonsense, but they are someone else's nonsense which should be treated with care.

I never imagined that one day I'd have a holy artefact in my own larder, hidden on the top shelf near the pineapple chunks and tinned pears, the stuff we'd eat in extremis. It's a small glass jar given to my wife by an Irish-American Catholic aunt. Inside are ten grapes in fluid. The grapes are said to have been blessed by the last Pope, John Paul II. The label has a dark tale to tell of the End Days: 'When the Pope leaves Rome there will follow three days of darkness when no one will be able to buy or sell food or leave their house. One grape, preserved in brandy, will sustain a person who believes it will for as long as is necessary.'

The scientist will say that the blessing was empty, the potency of the grapes dubious and that indeed they may well kill you. I say if anyone tries to take them from my larder, they'll have me to answer to.

The morning after I'd seen bits of the Three Wise Men, Stan and I woke up in our shared room reeking of cigars, lager and Brut. While Stan splashed it on all over in the bathroom, I leaned over our balcony and watched the morning sun illuminate the flying buttresses of the dark cathedral. After tucking into cold hams and cheeses we hit the autobahn.

Without the exhaust pipe over my right shoulder I had the freedom of the cab, and went hunting for a decent radio station on Stan's dial. I presented him with a number of choices, from Europop to Beethoven, but he was delighted when I found BBC Radio Two broadcasting across the northern continent on long wave. As a teenager sensitised to the nearest atom to what was the right music to be listening to, I could scarcely credit that Stan was prepared to travel back across Europe in the company of Jimmy Young.

We were steaming along the motorway well above any legal limit in Britain when the usually smooth and almost pathologically chirpy Jim pulled the needle off a record and told us he had a newsflash. He was very saddened to report the sudden death in Memphis, Tennessee of Mr Elvis Presley.

Stan braked hard and turned the volume up. He had heard right. The King was dead. Stan took his tinted glasses off and squeezed the bridge of his nose.

'Tell you what, Pauly, I think we might pull over for a minute.'

He slowed down more carefully and drew in to the hard shoulder, where we stopped. He got out of the car, walked up an embankment and sat on the grass. I began twiddling stations again to find they were either talking about Elvis in German or playing one of his songs, mostly Wooden Heart, a memory of his time serving in the U.S. Army in Germany, adapted from a folk tune in his film *G.I. Blues*.

I saw Stan's cigars on the dashboard and followed him up the grassy slope.

'Here you are, Stan.'

'Good lad. Will you join me?'

Of course, I would. Stan had things on his mind and out they came, his 'Love Me Tender' kisses with his then wife, the joy of the King and all his works.

'I can't believe he's dead.'

I was a hardened cigarette smoker by then, but I was careful not to inhale this choking cigar. We looked as if we were sending up smoke signals from our elevated spot, and soon we were not alone. Before long a line of cars and lorries had pulled over. Strangers began to talk, and Stan shuffled down the embankment to shake their hands and say 'Elvis', standing quietly among them as they remembered their hero in a language in which he only understood the word for carburettor.

When we drove on again, I told Stan all I knew. In the last few weeks a Capital Radio DJ, Roger Scott, had said prophetically, having seen Elvis's most recent Las Vegas concert, that he'd plainly needed very urgent medical help, as he looked like a sausage about to burst its skin. Scott had taken to overplaying Elvis's latest and worst song 'Way Down', and this had nearly driven us mad in a summer of punk.

Stan couldn't give a monkey's about this instant journalism.

'You wouldn't have seen his comeback in sixty-eight, Paul. He was like a god. I don't want to think of him after that. I'll always remember him like a god.'

As we crossed the channel on the ferry, the speakers played

Elvis non-stop, the hero of an era before mine, and Stan worked his way through packets of duty-free cigars with fellow mourners on their way back with juggernauts from distant lands. I spent a lot of the time on deck getting away from the racket and seeing to my tan, and wondering if one day hundreds of years hence, when his music was still played, a cathedral would house a sarcophagus containing the bones of this king.

Since that day in 1977, many have seen him, and thousands try to be him. Millions more have paid homage at his home. Forty-six countries have issued postage stamps. Never mind the Catholics, Elvis was a latter-day Hindu deity.

At the Crease

The Christian Church in Britain was about to stop being so boring. It had no alternative. The Archbishop of Canterbury was a whiskery sweetheart looking at a disturbed nation from under his bushy eyebrows. He connected with tea-room England perfectly. The constituency was people like my parents who took children to son-et-lumière shows outside his cathedral on wet June evenings, where the voices of ageing luvvies boomed from behind cut-outs of Thomas à Becket while we shivered.

Our middlebrow stoicism might have been the true pulse of the C of E, but it was not dealing with global reality in the late 1970s. Elsewhere in the Christian world there were priests as turbulent as Becket, possessed of all the courage the young wanted their Christ to represent, epochs away from the powder-puff version of Canterbury. In South Africa, Bishop Trevor Huddlestone was speaking out against apartheid at great risk to his life, and through his supporters back in London he arranged protests outside the South African embassy that went on until Nelson Mandela's release two decades later. This impressed those of us who took communion seriously, and on our way to the Odeon Leicester Square we'd stop by for a couple of verses of 'Fre-ee, Nelson Mandela'. Much of this political wing of Christianity was discussed at St James's Church on Piccadilly, which paid host to militant seminars and lectures, a conduit for the alternative faiths and cultures of the sixties, which gradually entered the mainstream.

Then, from within my own school, a courageous figure emerged, standing in brave opposition to our headmaster, a rugger-bugger whose amiable manner disguised a thin intellect.

It was mystifying that he considered it a good idea at that particular time to invite an all-white South African school team to play rugby against our first team. He waffled about 'bridge-building', but the whole thing whiffed of complacency.

As ever, he had underestimated the passion of the children in his care, and the captain of the first XV led a protest against having to play which eventually featured in the *Sunday Times*. The captain, along with five other members of the team, had the guts to have their photograph taken in school uniform to go alongside a pretty angry piece.

The captain was a clever young man, and he would have known that this protest could have cost him dearly. His whistle-blowing caused so much publicity that it seemed probable a demo of anti-apartheid campaigners would come to the playing fields of the school. Our proximity to tough areas like Brixton fed a concern that it would also lure a militia from the Anti Nazi League, a gang made up in equal quantities of well-intentioned softies and hardcore anarchists. The game was cancelled, and fifteen young men didn't have to spend the rest of their days wondering if it had been right to endorse the white regime in South Africa at the age of eighteen. For that, they had their captain to thank. His courage was rewarded by staff-room mutterings about loyalty and discretion.

Within the school's precincts, Christianity's profile was further boosted by a new chaplain, Tom Farrell, an ex-Olympic runner from Northern Ireland who became known as the faster pastor or the quicker vicar. He was not content to sit behind a pile of Latin books puffing a pipe like his predecessor, but rightly and swiftly identified that in a school of one and a half thousand children there were a fair few lost souls. To them he extended friendship and assistance, and he neither asked for nor expected any attendance at Christian gatherings in return. Everything he did was gentle, and he even influenced me on the running track, where one afternoon of kind suggestions did more for my times than years of being yelled at by old school P.E. teachers more suited to the barracks at Aldershot.

I liked him enormously, and felt sorry for him when he had to drink the dregs of communion wine on a Tuesday morning, a task which often seemed beyond him. Apart from universal kindness, his other characteristic was a determination to press on with good work as if no opposition to it existed. Some called this naivety, but I learned a lot from him in this regard. He didn't have a political fibre in his body, and almost without thinking he twice nearly caused a revolution in the conduct of our morning assemblies.

On the first occasion, he stepped up to the front of the stage in the Great Hall, leaving a long-haired guest sitting behind him in a smock.

'Hi there, boys,' he began in his gentle Irish burr. The headmaster winced. 'I'm not going to say anything more, except that I saw this gentleman speak a few months ago and I just knew I had to ask him to speak to you too. So here he is, then.'

The long-haired man came forward, closed his eyes, opened his palms to the room and without warning said, 'Blessed are the poor in spirit: for theirs is the kingdom of heaven.'

He looked down at us theatrically, which was apt, since he was an actor about to give us an electric rendition of the entire Sermon on the Mount, the speech given by Jesus at the peak of his powers when he was fresh in from the wilderness. There he'd resisted Satan for forty days and nights, and had then returned to the Sea of Galilee with thousands of new followers in tow, who he addressed on a hillside overlooking the lake.

The headmaster's brow wrinkled. Was this about to happen in one of his assemblies? It was.

The actor got into his stride, and before we knew it he was running about the stage, down the aisles, standing on chairs, sinking to his knees, weeping, yelling, imploring. He could have blown this, but he didn't. He was magnificent. He was a good performer, which helped, but he also had the advantage of complete surprise in a hall full of young men worrying about overdue homework. Most of all, to give credit where it is due, he had some of the best lines ever spoken to work with. This happens with Shakespeare, of course: one character says all the world's a stage, and you think what a genius playwright he must have been to have left great slices of verbal pie like this behind him. But Will had nothing on the Sermon on the Mount. You need only hear a sample of the expressions minted by Jesus in his ten minute soliloquoy which course through our vernacular today:

Salt of the earth. Good for nothing. Hiding your light under a bushel. Turning the other cheek. Don't blow your own trumpet. The left hand doesn't know what the right hand is doing. Don't point out the speck in your brother's eye and ignore the log (mote) in your own. Don't cast your pearls before swine. Seek and ye shall find. Do unto others as you would have them do unto you. Beware of false prophets in sheep's clothing. Don't build your house on sand. A corrupt tree brings forth evil fruit.

All of this spilled from the actor's lips in its King James Bible form, riper still with poetic phrasing as he bounded about the place like a monkey. Actors adore good speeches, and this was the peachiest ever written. It kicked off with that list of Blesseds, nine groups of the reviled and the dispossessed given recognition by the son of God. Then, just as it was flagging and those with a short attention span were shuffling in their seats, it produced the first ever statement of the Lord's Prayer, from 'Our Father, which art in Heaven' to 'for ever and ever. Amen'. There is quite a difference between hearing the Lord's Prayer muttered by bored school children and seeing it projected with the impact of a great oration.

The actor came to a climax and did that thing actors do – bowed his head in silence. The end. The headmaster stood up to say something, but was drowned out by the torrent of applause and cheering. He couldn't top what had just happened, so when we piped down he dismissed us. I think most had no idea what they'd just seen. They thought the actor was some plain-clothes vicar of the century who'd belted out a fantastic new sermon.

Woody wasn't sure either, and asked me about it as we walked back for a German class. I told him it was the Sermon on the Mount, and said that if he reckoned Jesus was just a minor prophet, he should think again. Woody was impressed, as if he'd just seen a really cool rock band play a secret gig.

That lunchtime Tom Farrell saw me in the dining hall and zipped across the room. I told him I thought the assembly had been stupendous. He was pleased but concerned that the headmaster hadn't said anything. He wouldn't have done, and neither would he have expected the Reverend Farrell's next trick.

A month or so later we were back in the same hall, and as the headmaster's party trooped up on to the stage we saw that they were followed up by a tall, middle-aged black man. The headmaster walked up to the lectern with a great big grin.

'Good morning, gentlemen. We have something of a treat in store for you this morning. I am delighted to say that we are joined by Mr Conrad Hunte. You will all remember Mr Hunte's legendary stand of 446 for the sixth wicket with Sir Gary Sobers against Pakistan.'

Almost none of us knew about that. Hunte had retired almost fifteen years earlier, so most of us weren't born when he was in his prime. However, those who knew their cricket were as excited as the headmaster. Here was a man who could tell us of his feats scoring centuries in a great West Indian XI against every country they'd played.

'I'm perfectly sure Mr Hunte will treat us to some super stories from his marvellous years at the crease.'

The headmaster sat down, smiling broadly, anticipating tales from the wickets of the world. Mr Hunte had something else in mind.

'Thank you, headmaster,' he said with a Barbadian lilt. 'You know, when the Reverend asked me here to speak to you boys today, I think he knew you'd all be as bored by my telling you about my batting average and so forth as I'd be by saying it. That was all a very long time ago.'

The headmaster's grin tautened.

'No, the best way I may serve gentlemen such as yourself is to tell you the real story about my life. There came a point some years ago when I was tired to my bones. I was all alone, and I remembered how my mother used to take me to church in Barbados, and how when I left home I had turned away from it. And I was so burdened with weariness that one day I said out loud, "Lord, will you have me back?" And the Lord did not answer. And I despaired.'

The headmaster's grip on the pleats of his gown tightened.

'And so I prayed. And I prayed and I prayed and I *prayed*. And only then did I understand. The Lord would not welcome me back into his home until I had repented. Do you hear what I am saying to you? Repented. Now, you young men may have little to repent for, but I did. *Oh Lord, I had much to repent.*'

Hunte walked away from the lectern and came closer to us.

'So much, I could not remember it all. So I made a list. And what I saw on that list was one great flaw in me from childhood to that very day. I was a thief. When I was a tiny boy I had stolen fruit from an old man's stall. I stole money to pay for my first bat. And that was just the beginning. Oh yes, the list went on and on until I wrote down the final item of my larceny. As Vice Captain of the West Indies cricket team, I had claimed many dollars in falsified expenses. I had cheated my own country's cricket board.'

The headmaster had given up trying to feign anything other than misery. His head hung low.

'And I sat down with that list in my hand and prayed, and for the first time I had an answer from the Lord. Not much. Two words. But I knew what he meant. Repay them. And that is what I did.

'I found every man, woman or child I had ever stolen from, no matter how little I had taken, and I repaid them. And I asked them to forgive me. And when this was done, without exception, I prayed again. "Now, Lord, willst thou have me?" And he answered me, yes. And I fell to my knees and I have walked his righteous path every day since then.'

He turned back to the teachers on the stage.

'And that, headmaster, is a more important thing to tell your pupils than any vain boasts of centuries I made or international caps I won.'

He sat down. No applause this time. More of a stunned silence. The headmaster rose to his feet.

'Well, Mr Hunte. I . . . most interesting. Not quite what we'd expected. Some of the older chaps might like to know, do you ever get a game of cricket these days?'

'I do.'

'Super.'

'For my church.'

'I see. Well that's all we have time for, I'm afraid. Off you go then, boys.'

Perhaps it was me. I felt his speech had been earth-shattering, a wonderfully frank confession within which was embedded a tale of active redemption. Nobody else seemed that bothered. Perhaps it was because in my pre-confirmation days I'd been a bit of a tea leaf myself, but I think I was just excited to realise that in the field of Christianity the devil didn't have to have all the best tunes.

I had just witnessed two emerging aspects of the church's fightback against apathy.

The first had been to throw away all sense of inhibition and get an actor in to make great speeches for you. This liberalisation of what passed for a church service was taking hold across the country. Anywhere the vicar wore sideburns, guitars and tambourines were taking the place of the organ. This was a sincere effort, noxious to the gauleiters of good taste, to make Christ's message more accessible.

The second, in the well-worked fire and brimstone of Conrad Hunte's address, was the germ of the black revivalist churches which would rescue swathes of south London in the decades to come. It was still early days, but communities in Peckham and New Cross were beginning to acquire old meeting rooms or dance halls and make not an hour but a whole day of church on Sunday.

Best clothes, best behaviour, astonishing singing and electrifying preachers.

It all promised so much more than the paralysed services at St George's. This wasn't mealy-mouthed. It was about words such as repentance and sin, praise and salvation. A year or two down the line I saw one of its natural outcomes, and didn't like that at all. But its energy was undeniable, compared to the lukewarm Anglicanism of my own tribe.

However, men like Tom Farrell were not prepared to give up either. Just around the corner something interesting lurked: a schism.

His Name Was Brian

Not being ordained, I don't know if the average vicar's life is more joy or woe. Does he really leave church after Mattins on a Sunday morning thinking how lucky he is to have another three or four services before bedtime? Or does he trudge back to the vicarage for a cuppa and a slice of toast, wishing he'd been a lumberjack? Tom Farrell was the first priest I ever knew as something approaching a friend, and his attitude to life seemed constantly to be in the glass half-full category. He expressed his happiness by a stream of good deeds; but his success in helping the needy arose from his common decency, formal Christianity taking second place.

In the late 1970s Tom suddenly became so animated with theological enthusiasm that it spilled out everywhere he went. One of his dreams, in common with many priests, had come true. A new translation of the Bible was to be published, originating from America and written in plain, modern English. The opening passage from the Second Book of Samuel, chapter 15 had always read thus:

> 1. And it came to pass after this, that Absalom prepared him chariots and horses, and fifty men to run before him. 2. And Absalom rose up early, and stood beside the way of the gate: and it was so, that when any man that had a controversy came to the king for judgement, then Absalom called unto him, and said, Of what city art thou?

The new translation read:

> After this, Absalom provided a chariot and horses for himself, and an escort of fifty men. He would get up early and go and

stand by the road at the city gate. Whenever someone came there with a dispute that he wanted the king to settle, Absalom would call him over and ask him where he was from.

The new version had been in the pipeline for a decade under the aegis of the American Bible Society. By 1976 it was ready to be published in Britain with a bright yellow cover bearing the name *The Good News Bible*. There were many for whom this shiny, happy arriviste was bad news, to be condemned. The Christian community of Dulwich, whose heads were usually filled with adverbs and worries over acne, were deliberately divided by two strong characters.

The Good News was Tom Farrell. The Bad News was a mannered English teacher named Fairlamb. Sparks flew.

Before that summer all the Bibles I had ever seen were printed on thin paper, bound in leather, and embossed with gold lettering. The edges of the pages facing outwards glittered with a layer of gold paint. There was a red tassel to mark your place, and twenty or so oil paintings printed with care on to thick paper showing Joseph before Pharaoh or Jesus turning over the money-lenders' tables in the Temple at Jerusalem. My copy would have been printed, but it gave the impression of something olde worlde, not least because it was written in 1611 by a committee of scholars and theologians commissioned by King James I.

The evolutionary tree leading to that settled version, which had prevailed for nearly four centuries, is complex and often disputed. There are archaeologists still scraping off layers of Middle Eastern earth hoping to find even earlier versions of the Bible than the ones we have, though the existing line of descent is surprisingly robust. The earliest gathering of the four gospels resides in the library at Dublin Castle, bequeathed by the American industrialist and mining engineer Chester Beatty. Written on papyrus in Greek, its origin is not certain but it probably came from an Egyptian monastery and was written in about 250 AD.

In the red-brick British Library in London, the fourth-century *Codex Sinaiticus* (the Book From The Sinai) still provides daily work for conservators, transcribers and computer wizards hoping eventually to disseminate it entirely through the Internet. For centuries it was preserved in St Catherine's monastery at the foot of Mount Sinai. Unlike the Chester Beatty, it is a complete New Testament (not just the four gospels), with some books of the Old Testament included too.

The first nation to officially adopt Christianity was Armenia, at the beginning of the fourth century, and the first book ever translated into Armenian was the Bible, which was known as Astuadsashuntchh or 'breath of God'. Syriac translations, from a dialect of eastern Aramaic spoken at the time of Christ, are extant from the fifth century, possibly in the language in which one or more of the gospels were first written. From the seventh century there are Coptic bibles, written in the Egyptian language with Greek letters.

The first effort to unite all the differing versions of the Old and New Testaments was commissioned by Pope Damasus I in 382 AD from Jerome, a rich young man born in Dalmatia and lavishly educated in Roman and Greek studies, who became a hermit in the Syrian desert of Chalcis for five years to concentrate more fully on his Christian faith. There he spent all his time reading the Scriptures and learning Hebrew until, at the age of forty-two, he returned to Rome, famous both for the breadth of his scriptural knowledge and for a scandal over his alleged ministrations to a group of merry widows wishing to pursue a more Christian life.

Under papal commission he spent the remainder of his days in a stone cell in Bethlehem making Latin translations of the New Testament from Greek and the Old Testament from the original Hebrew with Paula, one of the merry widows, for occasional company. He died thirty-eight years later having completed the Vulgate (or common version) of the complete Bible in Latin. It remained definitive for more than a thousand years, though some of the colourful aspects of his life gave him a reputation within the Church more suited to a writer than a divine.

The man who finally translated Jerome into English was Thomas Wycliffe, at the end of the fourteenth century, and as happened so often with the Bible, he was driven on by seismic shifts in the use of language. By the 1360s the old tongues of Anglo-Saxon and Norman-French were becoming fused into Middle English. This had become the language of the law courts and of the sermons, and in sections of the church liturgy it had begun to displace Latin.

Beyond his personal ambition to present a Bible in the language of the ordinary people, Wycliffe opposed corruption in the Church – what he saw as the degradation of the papacy. He loathed its sale of indulgences, by which remission of sins could be bought by the highest bidder, and its system of English bishoprics held by foreigners who never came near them, except to claim the revenues from their See. His greatest desire was to have a Bible in English free from interpretation by corrupt clerics, and he gave hundreds of handwritten texts to 'poor preachers' dressed in rough serge who spread through the countryside teaching that this was the direct word of God.

This appalled the Pope, who demanded that he be stopped and declared him a heretic. The Wycliffe Bibles were ordered to be burned, and he was exiled back to his home at Lutterworth in Leicestershire, where after two years he died. His bones were dug up forty years later and thrown into a river.

Wycliffe had been a century before his time. He is sometimes referred to as the 'Morning Star of the Reformation', and though use of his few remaining Bibles remained underground, his example was widely admired. A hundred years later, Martin Luther translated the Bible into German, a crucial influence on the great scholar William Tyndale, who had secretly been making an English Bible in the Cotswold village of Little Sodbury, not from the Latin of St Jerome, but from ancient Greek and Hebrew texts.

Terrified of the consequences of discovery, Tyndale came to London in 1523 to announce his project openly. He won patronage from Henry Monmouth, an alderman of the City, but was denounced by the Bishop of London. He realised that his best hope was to flee to Hamburg, where he finished his work, and then to Cologne, where he intended to have it printed, only to be betrayed. He had just enough time to snatch the galleys of his New Testament from the printing press and flee again to Worms.

The English bishops were horrified to hear that Tyndale had successfully printed and imported thousands of copies of his New Testament from Worms, and confiscated them wherever they could be found. Hundreds at a time were burned in front of St Paul's Cathedral, and friends and followers of Tyndale met a similar fate. Even as he was being condemned as 'the murderer of the truth' he turned his attention to the Old Testament, but he was betrayed in Antwerp and thrown into prison at Vilvorde near Brussels, where he was tortured, tried, strangled and then burnt at the stake.

A dialectic had emerged. Certain individuals believed they should strain every fibre to bring the Bible to the widest readership, while Church authorities, fearing unregulated browsing by a moronic flock, frantically repressed their efforts. The change in direction which finally permitted a Bible to be freely distributed in English arose from the marital difficulties of Henry VIII. At first he endorsed Tyndale's arrest. Then, realising the Pope would not grant him a divorce, he split from Rome and declared himself 'Head on Earth of the Church in England'. It was suddenly expedient for him to endorse a new English version.

This was written and published by Miles Coverdale working in voluntary exile in Zurich and Antwerp, drawing on German translations, the work of Tyndale, and Jerome's Latin Vulgate. Even as Tyndale was being burned at the stake, Henry permitted Coverdale's Bible to be published in England, with a dedication to himself and a massive etching on the title page of him sitting on his throne in the kind of position more usually allotted to Christ, all and sundry around him emitting speech bubbles saying 'Vivat Rex'. Each parish was ordered to keep one of these valuable 'Great' Bibles, so called because of their enormous size, chained to a desk or a stone wall.

Thousands read them, but within a few years even these were banned, torn from their mountings and burnt by followers of the Catholic Mary Tudor. Finally, in 1604, James I ordered yet another translation. Scholars in Westminster, Cambridge and Oxford drew on the Hebrew, Greek and Latin texts, as well as Tyndale's New Testament, and worked for seven years until in 1611 they presented King James's Authorised Version of the Bible to their king. And lo, he saw that it was good.

This is a long story, played out across many centuries, and omits the preservation of the texts in Lindisfarne and Kells, kept safe during the dark ages after the fall of Rome. It is concerned only with the written word, and not the rich illustrations added to them by devoted monks such as St Aidan and St Cuthbert, with their posse – Eadfrith, Ethelwold and 'Billfrith the Anchorite' who adorned the Book of Kells with gold and silver and gems and overlaid it with silver.

Then, one historically hot summer three hundred and sixty-five years later, a fogeyish English teacher was presented with the *Good News Bible* by a school chaplain. It was not written by Oxbridge scholars or illuminated by celibate monks, for whom he felt some empathy, but by theologians in the New World, and Fairlamb hated it. He did not feel obliged to back the school chaplain's enthusiasm.

Fairlamb came out screaming, in lessons, in assemblies, in vociferous discussions around the premises. It would be wrong for me to pretend that his anger was the talk of the playground, but for the minority of us with an active interest in the subject, it was like stepping into a time machine and witnessing the birth of a schism between two previously united members of the same Church. While Tom Farrell seemed to me to be following in the line of Wycliffe and Tyndall, at a time when the King James Bible was in large parts incomprehensible to the majority of people, Fairlamb felt its usurper was an insult to the historic journey which had yielded a holy book he adored.

To a fifteen-year-old he seemed at first quite mad as he droned on about the 'poetry' of the King James compared with the infelicitous prose of the *Good News*. (To us, good poetry rhymed and preferably began 'There was an old lady from Ealing/Who had a peculiar feeling'.) Tom Farrell was so animated by the *Good News* that he confessed it had cleared up misunderstandings even he'd had as a trained priest. Fairlamb's arguments seemed like waffle about mysteries and so forth; his sub-text was that if you weren't educated enough to understand the King James then that was your look-out.

It shouldn't have mattered, but suddenly it did. Which Bible was going to be used on the termly trip to chapel? Was it to be the reading from the old St John? – 'In the beginning was the Word, and the Word was with God, and the Word was God' – or the Good News St John? – 'Before the world was created, the Word already existed; he was with God, and he was the same as God.'

This was difficult. The new version made a kind of sense, but if you were projecting it from a lectern, the older version of this key passage was vastly more appealing and won hands down. One was like Shakespeare in the original, the other like the bowdlerised Lamb's tales.

But the distinction went deeper than that. Tom Farrell had a faith, a belief, and he needed as a tool a text which would help him spread it about in plain English. The likes of Fairlamb seemed to have something more sophisticated going on. Who in their right mind, they might argue, could possibly believe the Bible was the literal truth? Nobody. So what it was about, above all else, was an expression of some holy spirit through the power of myth, story, parable, teaching and, *pace* St John, the Word. And looking at it like this, nobody could insist that the prosaic words of the Good News weren't the country cousins of the genuine articles in the King James.

I loved this debate. I was still paying heed to pop music, football, girls, the *News at Ten* and all the other fabric of daily life. But here, in front of me, was a dispute. In one corner was a gentle, good priest who drove fallen, alcoholic teachers into school every day just to give them hope, and in the other was a self-regarding bachelor who liked rolling the ancient text around in his mouth like a humbug. My heart backed Tom Farrell, but I repressed a loud voice in my head which would have voted, when push came to shove, for King James.

I was not privy to how this affair played out in the teachers' common room, whether it was conducted in coffee-breathed chats at first break or hair-pulling and fisticuffs after hours. I just liked the glow of it, and then, after a couple of years of wrangling, just as the flames began to die down, along came another schism from the outside world. This time it was me cast as the revolutionary and Tom Farrell as the reactionary. It's name was Brian. *The Life of Brian*.

Caution must be exercised in describing the work of Monty Python's Flying Circus. Like Whaley's Goon impressions, play-ground re-enactments of the previous night's Python risked proving a deficit of wit. I saw no reason to despise the happy clusters of pupils doubled-up with mirth doing their Eric Idle voice. Know what I mean, know what I mean? However, the feature film of *Brian* is a special case, the most fully realised satire in British comedy which, like the latter-day masterpiece *Team America*, spared nobody's feelings. Without bothering to go and see the film, its opponents smeared it as a deliberate blasphemy against Christ.

This misreading was plainly stupid. Two of the earliest scenes depict Jesus as a background figure, once at his birth and next as he gives the Sermon on the Mount, where squabbling onlookers wonder why he has said, 'Blessed are the cheesemakers', only to be corrected by a smart-arse saying they should not take this literally but as an indication that God favours makers of all dairy products. It's an oft-cited scene, creating clear water between the

life of Christ and the life of Brian, while simultaneously lampoon-
ing the preposterous semantic debates of theology from that day
to this.

There are good reasons why my generation loved this film
immediately. Our world then seemed as mad as any we had read
about, and it skewered so many of the causes of our discontent:
trade union negotiators, splinter terrorist groups, Catholic and
Protestant maniacs in Northern Ireland, false prophets, denoun-
cers of blasphemy, upper-class twits and Latin teachers.

When Brian was swept off the planet briefly by an alien craft it
opened another front against the voguish trend of the time for
science fiction films and books offering half-baked explanations
of humanity coming from other planets or universes. There were
great steaming dollops of this nonsense, from ludicrous tomes
claiming that Inca mountaintops were landing strips for aliens, to
the astonishing waste of money spent trying to prove that a
radioactively awakened Christ in his tomb had deposited a
negative image of himself on the Turin shroud.

Finally it somehow satirised the very form it was made in,
mocking the biblical epic output of Hollywood which had been
killing us with boredom since the war – anything with Victor
Mature or Charlton Heston gnashing their teeth, and our coun-
trymen Charles Laughton or Peter Ustinov relegated to fatso
villains. These films were nonsense which flowed from the
strange mixture of piety in the Judeo-Christian mix running
the Hollywood studios hoping to be the next D.W. Griffith,
their proximity to a perfect stand-in for the Holy Land, the
Californian desert, and the new technology of technicolor which
seemed at first best suited to the epic form.

One lunchtime, Tom Farrell was inflating a flat tyre on his car
and I parked my bum on the bonnet for a chat. With complete
innocence I recommended that he go and see *The Life of Brian*. He
stopped pumping immediately.

'What are you saying, Paul? Don't tell me you've been to see it.'

His face registered total shock, as if I'd corrupted my soul.

'No, it's all right, Tom. It's brilliant.'

'Oh dear no.' He put his hand on my forearm. 'Please, Paul, don't tell anyone else you've been. For everyone's sake.'

Damn, another hero with feet of clay. He was almost the only person I knew who hadn't seen it. I felt it was my duty as his friend to tell him he really should go. It was clearly going to become a landmark in film-making with a religious context. But Mary Whitehouse had got to him, and anyway he had another area of showbusiness in mind. A few weeks later he hosted a school from Connecticut who used our ramshackle theatre to stage a production of *Godspell*. The young men were bearded and the young women wore diaphanous dresses, their huge crinkly hair parted in the middle, and they sang to us, 'Prepare Ye the Way of the Lord' and 'I Don't Know How to Love Him' like they really meant it. Unbeknownst to us, America had diagnosed the Christian deficit and moved on. *Songs of Praise* would have been cancelled by an American TV executive after the first transmission. They had something else in the airwaves.

I'd always known that I did not belong with the boys of the Christian Union, and it saddened me that their official policy was to boycott the film, in a mistaken parody of the boys with real Christian courage who had boycotted the rugby game against South Africa. It was then that I began to realise how broad a church must be if it is not to fragment.

The Christian Union had started giving out little plastic stickers, like the ones Peter had filched for me at St George's, with a white outline symbol of a fish. This fish represented the first secret signal between Christians in Rome. Greek for fish is *ichthys*, which was then taken to stand for *Iesos Christos Theou Yios Soter*. Jesus Christ, Son of God the Saviour. The boy who'd led me to the cane was very excited about this and drew fish all over his exercise books.

I saw this one afternoon and walked away muttering under my breath, for nobody's ears in particular, my own secret code: 'Oh, for f—'s sake.'

The Reclining Buddha

I'd have been a hopeless colonial administrator in the British Empire. Any Foreign Office mandarin would have spotted my potential for going native at the first interview. Highly unlikely to be trusted to don the rhino hide of the imperialist in dealing with civilisations different to my own, I would have failed utterly as a collector of taxes or major domo to a Maharaja of strategic importance. In a fortnight I'd be in a dhoti, in a month I'd be married to a princess, and within a year I'd be dead from malaria.

What I would have been okay at is the journey out there. Others might have been playing deck games and bridge; I would have been bad company at both. My place would have been at a tiny desk in my cabin reading as many books as I could find on the place I was about to land in. When, on arrival, an upper-class twit demanded why some blighter would not shake him by the right hand, I would be able to tell him why.

Such opportunities for shipboard learning between continents began to vanish with the airplane. When I was travelling with a representative party from my school to Asia for the first time, the fortnight I might have relied on to read about the origins and history of Buddhism in Sri Lanka were shrunk to the flight from Heathrow to Dubai and then on to Colombo.

There were three particular reasons why the atmosphere in the cabin was not conducive to learning. Since we were flying Singapore Airlines, whose exotic TV commercials then outdid those for Fry's Turkish Delight, my companions' heads span lustfully as the supposedly beautiful hostesses trolleyed down the aisles. Making things even less bookish, these ladies were dispensing free drink. To eliminate any possibility at all of my spending some quiet moments with Buddha, my companions these representatives, were something else too. They, we, were a touring rugby team.

A general unreadiness for any spiritual discovery in our journey ahead became clear on the brief stopover at Dubai. I found the minarets, the women in niqabs and the calls to prayer as affecting as the desert oven drying my eyes, but this just seemed to make the rest of the team strut a bit higher. I would have succumbed to the strangeness then and there, but they were ready for a scrum-down and ready to teach a good lesson to anyone who dared question their pink-skinned presence far from home.

What I needed was a long solo voyage in steerage to negotiate the difference between south London and the mainly Buddhist world I was flying to. Even in the late seventies, much of our perception was shaped by what was presented to us on TV. The first Buddhist image I ever saw was a monk protesting cross-legged in the middle of a road in Vietnam. He had just set himself on fire. It was probably the first death broadcast in Britain, and certainly the most horrific. When unwell, one also caught up with the meagre offerings of afternoon television, featuring *Crown Court*, Mavis Nicholson, and the incongruous spectacle of tele-vised yoga. For reasons of religious impartiality, no proper explanation was given for this during the programmes. I had no idea why bearded men and bony-hipped women from High-gate elected to tie themselves in knots with strangely serene faces before a confused nation.

Woody, of course, was years ahead of the rest of us in Eastern practices, taking part in Transcendental Meditation classes in Herne Hill and refusing to tell us the secret word he had to focus on to make it all go with a swing. I was sure then and surer now that he hadn't a clue what he was playing at and that there was probably a young woman at the bottom of it.

That I was heading to Sri Lanka and Thailand on a rugby tour was curious. I was too young for the team, and, other than an ability to get from A to B quicker than nearly anybody else, I wholly lacked an appetite for what is called, with understatement, the physical side of the game. I was glad to be going, of course, and felt immensely privileged, but I wasn't really sure what I was doing there. This gradually became clear. In a tour of a dozen games or so, heads would be crushed and fingers snapped. I was there to make up the numbers. On less important fixtures I too had the opportunity to be stamped on by one hundred and ninety-two individual rugby studs after being caught in possession of the ball by a terrified Sri Lankan.

The Sri Lankans were right to fear us. In the tradition of English sportsmen overseas, we found one thing we were good at and did it repeatedly. The Sri Lankans were quicker and better handlers of the ball, two aspects of the brutal game which I respected. Unfortunately for them they did not breed gigantic eighteen-year-old ginger boys called Ed. Our strategy, to our shame, was to get the ball to Ed and watch as he literally ploughed through Sri Lankan flesh. He scored most of our tries, a red-faced Samson with five or six tiny Sri Lankans hanging round his neck as he fell over the line like a shot rhinoceros. It was a scene less suitable for this serendipitous island in the Indian Ocean than to some fiery battle between gods in the Hindu *Mahabharata*.

My estrangement from these unworthy games was the perfect soil for some self-taught Buddhism, for the first Buddha was himself a privileged man made restless by unhappy sights. As we progressed from Colombo up into the hills of Kandy and the Temple of the Sacred Tooth, I made more headway into the only book I'd found in the Dulwich library which spoke of the host country's religion. It appealed to a sixteen-year-old because it gave labels and meaning to a range of feelings of self-awareness typically blossoming at that age, and like so many religions it began with a plausible story.

Five hundred years before Christ, by which time the Indian subcontinent had possessed its main Hindu texts for two millennia, a high-born prince named Siddharta Gautama was born in Lumbini in today's Nepal. His mother died a week after she'd given birth to him, and when his father consulted a sage called Asita he was told that his son was destined to be the Enlightened One. His father realised that those who turned to religion usually did so out of the experience of human suffering, and so he raised his child within the confines of his palace in the greatest of luxury. It's a highly sympathetic beginning to a life – a boy who never knew his mother protected by his father's love.

Unlike Peter Pan, Siddharta had to grow up. He married, took a share of concubines, and like any rich young man with a brain felt overwhelming pangs of curiosity about the world outside the palace walls. He began to make a series of forays in which his naivety about human life was exposed. He saw an old man, a dying man and a dead man and realised that all these conditions were waiting in store for him too.

Many rich young men might have retreated to the concubines, but Siddharta had seen a sadhu from the shramana tradition – not a well-heeled priest of the Brahmin caste, but a scruffy itinerant monk. So he shaved off his hair, studied with the wisest scholars of the Hindu texts, slept in the jungle on a bed of thorns, starved himself nearly to death, and began the practice of controlling his breath to the point almost of extinction. Realising that neither this tough regime nor palace life were giving him any answers, he sensibly developed a Middle Path, and sat down under a bhodi tree until he had worked it all out.

The more mythological version of events tells of his mental fight beneath the tree with Mara, a Buddhist Satan, who had at his disposal an army of elephants and a troupe of beautiful daughters. The account favoured in the West by the late 1970s was more psychological. Siddharta's deep meditation brought him to a state of what he considered complete knowingness. He remembered former existences, he understood that bad deeds in one carried over to the next, and he saw clearly the traits which led to them: sensual desire, the desire to live, ignorance, and clinging to set views and ideas. The net effect was a realisation that the idea of 'I' had to be removed from centre-stage, and man had to make himself at one with everything around him. Wised up in this way, when Siddharta looked up at the morning star from his mattress of leaves under the tree near Patna, he had become the *Buddha*, the Awakened One.

To me, a fish out of water on a surreal rugby tour, this was a good read. There were some big egos knocking about in our team, especially in the scrum, and I felt most of them could do with some time in the jungle themselves. As I read further it made even more sense. It seemed that after his enlightenment the Buddha had come up with the first self-help manual: Three Universal Truths, Four Noble Truths and the Eightfold Path.

The Eightfold Path particularly interested me, just as it fascinated thousands of others in the West looking for spiritual guidance in a post-Christian climate. In essence the Eightfold Path was the young nephew to the Ten Commandments and the wise uncle to the Sermon on the Mount, but with a magic ingredient which seemed to lift the curse off taking one's religion seriously. There was no God. There was no requirement to believe in a Maker, a Saviour, or a Holy Spirit. It was all about enlightenment and oneness in the individual. With meditation, one still had the advantage of a method similar to our use of prayer, but with knobs on. Buddhists didn't sit stiffly on wooden benches in their Sunday best. They wore loose clothes with their legs folded, hands nicely poised, and their breathing under control.

Rugby coaches think differently this century: they hire yoga teachers to give their players flexibility and strengthen their core. In the side-burned seventies, sitting on a tour bus with my book on Buddhism marked me out as a suspicious character. What this team needed, the view prevailed, was not a namby-pamby soft-boy casting admiring glances at monks in saffron robes and counselling right speech, right action, and right work to a perplexed prop-forward. On this unholy vehicle, songs were sung which blasted all hope of this into oblivion – the repeated 'Four and Twenty Virgins', for example, with its barbaric punchlines on the theme of abortion, circumcision or missionary coitus performed in the standing position. The further into the tour we got, the more distance grew between me and my fellow thug.

I was going through a classic encounter of West meets East. I'd boned up on a new subject and now felt something like contempt for the unenlightened ones in my company. I was a long way from home, and everything Buddhist seemed more right with every mile.

Then I was confronted with reality. First, temptation, with particular reference to desire. My struggle with this came at a point when I was well on the road to going native. I floated into Trincomalee on a cloud of self-righteousness. Even the world seemed to be moving against my unenlightened comrades. All the way from Colombo, one of the principal coach-party singers had behaved like a dog seeing its master open a can of Pedigree Chum, endlessly repeating how he was going to jump straight off the coach and run into the sea with his clothes on. He even sang 'I do like to be beside the seaside', driving players less aware of the need for right-mindfulness than me half mad. Duly, when the coach pulled up at a complex of beach huts next to the palm-fringed, azure sea of every Indian Ocean brochure, the young man jumped off the bus leaving his luggage behind, ran into the sea as promised, and stepped straight on to the spines of a waiting jellyfish. His howling reminded some of us of the noise the boy with the twisted testicles had made, and many of the faces watching as the ambulance pulled away were set in smirks rather than sadness.

I was above all that, but I could not avoid temptation in its next shape. Trincomalee was a remote spot, and the place we were staying seemed to be ours alone. Lying on the deserted beach later that afternoon with three other players, I was surprised to see three young blonde women walking toward us from about half a mile to the north. The closer they came in the rising waves of heat, the more certain I became that they weren't, after all, wearing white bikini tops with pink buttons and yellow triangular bottoms, that they were in fact stark naked and coming our way. The shock was threefold. We thought this paradise was ours alone. The other residents were female. They did not wear clothes.

As they passed right by us, we flipped on to our fronts out of necessity, and when they'd gone we were so astonished as to be for once beyond vulgar remarks. This was more than lust. This was a kind of vision. It was made more perfect, or imperfect if, like me, one was approaching a state of raised consciousness, when we saw that the walkers were eating from the same buffet table as us later on. Germans, *natürlich*.

This was the kind of visitation that Mara might have sent the Buddha, and beneath our mosquito nets that night many of us found sleep came only fitfully. I remember staring at the fan revolving above my head and wondering how powerfully Buddha would have had to strive not to be looking forward to the buffet breakfast and another long day on the beach. With a measure of hypocrisy, I polluted my consciousness twice the next morning, once goggle-eyed on the sands with my fellow voyeurs, and then alone later with the first chocolate I had found in a fortnight, an orange flavoured Lanka bar from the refrigerator of the beachside café.

By that evening, however, my progress in Buddhism was back on track. It made so much sense to a young man uncertain of the world. I am not Buddhist now, and never was, but of the ideas in the Eightfold Path there was one which preoccupied me at the age when I was trying to work out what to do with my life, and which stayed with me beyond Sri Lanka. Path Five – Right Livelihood, the idea that you should not do work which you know would do harm – an idea of denial of action taking into account the connectedness of everything.

The bug took stronger hold when we headed east away from fleshy Trincomalee and saw how the religion and the environment seemed to be in real harmony at Anuradhapura, where I circumambulated the white bell-shaped stupas holding statues of Buddha, and felt genuine awe in the ruins of a city-state which had crumbled before the Norman Conquests.

At Polonnaruwa, to the south, I tickled the granite toes of the immense Buddhas, and made the obvious contrast between the peaceful last moments of the Reclining Buddha, lying down with a full tummy ready to enter nirvana, and the final minutes of Christ, suspended from a wooden cross by nails driven into his palms.

At the ancient fort of Sigirya I did my own form of breathing exercise when I sprinted up its narrow path to the summit and stood panting but vividly alive, looking over a lush forest filled with whooping monkeys and many ways in which a careless Buddhist leaving the security of where I stood could die.

When we arrived back at the tour base in Kandy, the town was decorated for a feast day and all the local elephants were being hosed and scrubbed and adorned in henna. As night fell the screeching of untuned instruments crescendoed across the lake and lines of monks began to process up the steps into the Temple of the Tooth to pay their respects to one of the Buddha's molars. As in Cologne and everywhere else in Christendom where relics can be found, so in Asia too. It is a powerful concept even amongst atheists – think of the sentimental storage of a baby tooth for example, or a lock of hair stored alongside the first school report. At worst it seems harmless, an expression of fond respect.

The next morning I had a strange encounter with veneration. We'd finished a rugby training session at an extraordinary ground surrounded by jungle on both sides and weren't due back at the hotel immediately. I went into one of the empty open stands and sat quietly with my eyes closed and shirt off. I breathed in and out, untrained, of course, but getting the point, and as my lungs quietly filled and emptied, a sense of calm replaced the stupid exertions of being knocked over by Ed in a practice tackling session. I didn't say Om, but as my neck relaxed I could hear my own breath, and as I focused on this I became aware of another sound in the silence. It was as if a group of people were shuffling towards me along the bench seat, and padding up from behind.

I opened my eyes and saw that five or six Sri Lankans had

materialised in the seats on either side of me, with ten more to the rear and another dozen below. What they seemed to want to do was stroke my hair, smile at me and point out to each other the colour of my north European blue eyes. Whether they thought they were priceless jewels or just plain freaky I couldn't tell, but for ten minutes I was surrounded, basking in their beatific gaze under the sun.

It occurred to me that all I had to do was go with the flow. If similarly approached by strangers in Dulwich Park, a fight would have broken out within a minute. These people seemed merely curious and at peace, the young men with fresh moustaches linking arms and resting heads on each other's shoulders, not in a homo-erotic way but simply feeling less enclosed by the rules of personal space.

Of course I liked it. I was sixteen. I reckoned I looked pretty good. So they wanted to slightly worship me. Where was the harm in that? I liked this country, and I liked its religion, and other than the celibacy rule I could perfectly well see how I might not get back on the plane to face my A level year and work my way swiftly up to being a well-respected abbot in a *sangha*.

Nothing, however, is permanent. The next morning we headed up-country, and I met someone who began to change my mind.

Our next match was to be somewhere called Nuwara Eliya, to the south of Kandy. It looked about two hours away on the map, but took six, ever ascending, leaving the heat and dust behind, until we drove across a vast dam. We stopped to look over the edge and then ascended some more. This was tea country, and it was coldly drizzling like an April day in London. The roads narrowed, the drops over the edge became more terrifying, and we were introduced to a new shade of green glistening in the rain, speckled with the tiny yellow shapes of workers picking tea in plastic raincoats. Finally, near the summit, we drove into a little town. Nuwara Eliya was expecting us. There was merry waving as we passed down the main street and up a driveway to the Teaplanters' Club. This was not really Sri Lanka at all; it was Surrey, somewhere near Haslemere.

The club-house was half-timbered. Its gardens bloomed with red and pink roses. We were served tea, which had been grown, plucked, dried and cut within a few miles of the club, and many of us had cucumber sandwiches minus the crust for the first time. Replete, we headed to the dressing rooms, which had been furnished and laid out when Accrington Stanley were a force to be reckoned with. The air was soon rank with Ralgex and other stinging embrocations, and in our blue and black shirts we sprinted out on to the pitch.

Our previous opponents had been flyweight schoolboys of roughly our own age. Facing us today were a meaty team of Buddhas, none of whom would see thirty again. We were the flyweights now. When the game kicked off, our only weapon, flame-haired Ed, ran into a wall of solid blubber. He was lifted from his feet and driven backwards until the whole sorry circus lost its footing and was embedded in deep mud. I don't remember the score. Not much on our account, for sure. Afterwards we mingled with our oppressors, and I learned that when the British tea-planters had left the old Ceylon after the Second World War, an upper echelon of native people had stepped into their shoes, plantations, houses, clubs and entire way of life. Soon the shock of the defeat passed and with all tongues loosened by their favourite drink, Scotch, we settled in to an evening of food from the fifties – Brown Windsor Soup, Saddle of Lamb and Queen of Puddings.

At the evening's end I was driven by a 'boy' of fifty to my quarters at a tea-planter's house. My host was Charlie, and after breakfast the next day he walked me up the hill to his processing plant, where a tasting display had been set up in my honour. I could discern no difference between the three cups of fresh brew which Charlie encouraged me to roll around my mouth and spit into a bucket. They all seemed uniformly excellent, and when we left he gave me three huge caddies of premium grade leaves to take home. Showing off now, he drove me around the plantation in his rickety Land Rover, and as we approached the pickers I commented that they looked ethnically different to the Sri Lankans back in Kandy.

'Tamils,' said Charlie. 'Their people came across the Elephant Pass to Jaffna many years ago. Mainly they live in the north. They've laboured for this plantation for more than a century.'

He told me this confidently enough, but he seemed to be holding something back, and drove us back down to the house for a game of billiards.

'So then, Paul, what do you think of my country?'

It's the same the world over, any time, any place. Ask a sixteen-year-old boy what he thinks about something and he'll make the mistake of telling you. It's possible that an English schoolboy offered this opportunity is the single most patronising phenomenon on Earth.

So I told him how lucky he was. How great Buddhism was too. What a paradise he lived in. Then I asked him a question of Buddhist doctrine and he politely advised me that he couldn't possibly answer the question. He was not a Buddhist.

'Oh,' I said.

'I was raised a Christian.'

'I see.'

'You'll probably know that the British were here once?'

'Yes.'

'And also the Portuguese. And the Dutch. This is in many ways a very Christian country.'

He knocked a few yellow balls in swiftly and then leant against the table.

'I'm not saying I am a Christian, though, Paul. The distinction I wished to make was that I was not raised as a Buddhist.'

I felt a bit dim. I'd over-egged the Buddhist bit to the extent that I couldn't see how I could now express my genuine interest in his Christian background.

'When I was in England,' he said, 'my feeling was that most people didn't believe in anything any more. I found this most attractive. The English gave us their language and their administration. It is a pity they could not stay long enough to make Sri Lanka as secular a place as England is now.'

Over lunch he developed his theme. He told me that the Tamil workers were Hindu, and that the Hindus had many gods. He said that in his view Buddhism was just a breakaway faith, like Methodism, and at heart it was very close to Hinduism. He made the point that when we'd travelled up to the house in the darkness the night before, his driver had offered a prayer first to a little Buddha on the dashboard. The Buddhism I had read about, and which was practised in the West, was clean and lean, but if I stayed for long in Sri Lanka I'd soon see that it was as infested with idols and mumbo-jumbo as anything else.

I patronised him some more.

'But it's such a beautiful, peaceful county,' I said. 'You can feel a Buddhist serenity wherever you go.'

'I'm afraid my Tamil pickers might disagree,' he said, an idea which was beyond me for the moment as a servant brought in a bowl of lychees.

'It has always interested me,' he said, 'that the Buddha has got away with founding a religion from an act of utter selfishness.'

'Did he?'

'Why does nobody ever ask what happened to the wife and children he left behind in the palace? I may be very old-fashioned, but I believe that a sense of loyalty is more valuable than the hunt for personal enlightenment. I wonder if this is why his religion is meeting with such approval in the West.'

Later that night, after we'd all been down to the club again for a blistering session on the Scotch, he and I collapsed into leather armchairs, looking from his study up towards a panoply of stars. He was the most genial companion, and struggling to his feet he turned on a mono record player.

'We can get all the latest hits in Colombo,' he said. 'Have you heard of *Hotel California*?'

I had. It had been out for at least two years. As the stylus dropped on to track one, I looked at Charlie, who was imagining himself on a dark desert highway, cool breeze in the air. He sat down heavily in his chair.

'Do you know the work of Arthur C. Clarke?' he asked. 'He lives not far from here.'

Then Charlie, tea-planter and lapsed Catholic, began to tell me what he really believed in. Out it all spilled. Charlie's inner life was dominated by theories about alien life forms and robots from outer space, how men like Hitler were a manifestation of an evil force in the universe seeded by time travellers eons earlier. Bar taking the Eagles off the turntable and spinning 'Calling Occupants of Interplanetary Craft' by the Carpenters, he could not have given, to my mind, a more bonkers explanation of the meaning of life.

The more he went on, the more it sounded like a galactic melange of Hinduism, Buddhism and science fiction. What it most certainly was not was Christian, and, under a night sky as dotted with stars as I had ever seen, I suddenly felt very proud of the gentle, sceptical, ineffectual Anglicanism of my lukewarm English home.

Home would have to wait. From Sri Lanka we were flying further east to play even more rugby in Thailand. The Thai Theravada Buddhism was descended from the same line, but the temples and pagodas of Bangkok were made of burnished gold. The monks seemed less easy-going than in Sri Lanka, closer to the martial artists of *Kung Fu* on the television than their counterparts, who looked as though they literally would not hurt a fly. Like all religious traditions, Buddhism here had adapted to its environment. Further north in the Himalayas it was dominated by shamanism and astrology, but in Thailand it was purer. These monks really were striving not to be reincarnated ever again.

My sense of detachment from many of my fellow players deepened when a hairy cluster of them spent nights in sex shows and chucked away their virginity in massage parlours. There was laughter, but it was bleak and desperate and, by now, decades later, surely to god the occasion of some regret.

After seeing a shaven-headed pupil of the King's School Bangkok so obsessed to get the ball that he dived horizontally into a post, opening his scalp like a blood orange, I decided this was no longer the game for me. The theory was that big lads let off steam in rugby which might otherwise manifest itself in polite society. I no longer bought that idea. This game was little more than brute force in the guise of a sport. Enough.

Back in England I went on holiday with my parents to Sheringham in Norfolk, where the sand was colder than Colombo's, and apparently I talked loudly in my sleep. With the beginning of the next term I was in my final year at school, and in free study lessons I read in *The Times* of the civil war breaking out in Sri Lanka, the Tamil bombing of department stores and school buses, the dreadful reprisals of the Sri Lankan army.

I've continued to keep abreast of the conflict until the present day. To some, it is one war amongst many which prove the evil divisiveness of religion. I disagreed then and now. The conflict, like in the north of Ireland, is really about land and civil rights and tribalism. It is about the post-colonial settlement too, a sideshow unresolved since Indian independence in 1947. Above all, it is something that flows from science, not religion – the invention and manufacture of armaments.

The catastrophic proliferation of weaponry in the twentieth century was the awful by-product of amorality in science. Churches may have become cheerleaders during war in the patriotic interest, but their founding principle, which was often stated, was that violence is wrong. To sharpen their message, they said it was a sin. As a young sixth former who'd grown up watching the Aldermaston Marches and would soon have a girlfriend at the Greenham Common Women's Peace Camp protesting against the deployment of cruise missiles, I was all at sea on this. I could not understand why arms manufacturers weren't closed down. I learned how complex this issue was that autumn when my mother responded happily one evening to a news item on a deal to sell weapons to Saudi Arabia.

'Oh good,' she said, 'that should help with my Racal shares.'

I hadn't known she had any shares. In the sixth form centre the next day I looked up Racal in *The Times*. Electronic Communications, apparently, but not the kind they'd used in Poppa's radiograms. These were for every military purpose from communications in armoured cars to radars on aircraft carriers. Great. I, pacifist, was living partly off the 'defence' industry. What would George Bernard Shaw have written about that?

As I stood alone on Sydenham Hill station in the September air, staring into the dark tunnel under Crystal Palace hill, where the metal dinosaurs still basked in the Indian summer, it occurred to me that what Sri Lanka needed was another Middle Path, between the passive aggression of the Buddhist forces and the caste-obsessed militancy of the Hindu Tamils.

What surprised me most of all was that such a code already existed, to do with turning the other cheek and loving thy neighbour as thyself.

In the London twilight, Buddhism seemed less about enlightenment and more about the denial and suppression of oneself. A fast train roared from the tunnel towards me, and I knew it to be true that if ever I was going to wrestle with a religious life, it would be with the one right under my very nose.

Exodus

Anyone who has felt some warmth towards their school will recognise the feeling: after nearly a decade in the same place, an epic seems suddenly to be drawing to a close. My four closest friends today were made back then, and we hated and loved the place in varying degrees. As the curtain approached we shared the experience of school-leavers everywhere as, in the final months, everything started to feel small. More brutally, we had grown too big.

A problem for me in those final days was that, while I was still praying – not in a demented way but a sort of directed meditation in private – I knew this would seem to the rest of my world to be unsustainable and absurd. This argument was powerfully supported by repeated experiences as the seventies ground to a halt.

Personally, there was the day the Jehova's Witnesses lied to my father at our front door, insisting that they'd left a Bible at our house for me to read, and had to see me. I heard this from my room and stormed down the stairs, confronting them with their outright lie. Butter would not have melted in their mouths, but Peter sent them away with a flea in their ears. I was very impressed by his directness, and yet again I could see he wouldn't be an insurance assessor to be trifled with if you tried slipping a fraudulent motor claim past him.

It was hard to be liberal and unconcerned in the face of door-to-door salesmanship of this kind. Somehow these apparently meek people from Orpington had swallowed an American idea that since 1914 Satan had ruled the Earth. By poring over every word of the literally true Bible and obeying its every utterance, 114,000 of them, or us if I joined too, would be saved to reign with Christ in Heaven.

It can be tempting to take the line of least resistance with sects like this and just say 'Each to his own'. But a combination of their insane refusal to accept blood transfusions and their double-glazing-sales-style harassment of suburban homeowners was a step too far. Their blood complex came from a verse in chapter 17 of Leviticus, which is followed by the notorious chapter 18, infamously cited by those who cannot accept that homosexuals are born, not made, as biblical support for their unkind prejudice. Reading the Bible always struck me as a good idea, but the new mania for 'studying' it with blinkers on was taking groups like the Orpington Jehovas away from the benevolence of the New Testament and nearer the edge of a theological cliff.

I've often thought that I was lucky to be brought up in a suburban home which resembled a unique blending of Alan Ayckbourn and Harold Pinter, where there was as much primitive myth-making as on any South Sea island. One Sunday, another of our vast extended family came to lunch, a feast my mother prepared with immense skill. With the robin tweeting outside on the holly bush, this recently widowed elderly lady put down her fork and, as we chomped on our roast pork, filled the silence in her rural Essex accent.

'I have nothing to fear from the other side. I have seen Armageddon, but my time has not yet come. My John is there waiting for me.'

Betty carried on chewing some crackling while I looked round for the crew from *Candid Camera*. The lady saw that neither of us had really grasped what she'd just said.

'Peter understands what I'm saying, don't you, Peter?'

My father nodded and refused to catch my eye. After she'd gone, I asked him what the hell that was about. His unidentified High Church ancestor had mentioned Armageddon in one of his sermons, not as a video game but as the Hebrew for the Hill of Megiddo in Palestine, where the Book of Revelation says some great battle will be waged between Satan and God. The Bahá'í Faith got into a tangle over this when an actual Battle of

Armageddon was fought in 1918, and the British, led by Allenby, defeated the Ottoman Turks, which wasn't quite how they'd expected things to play out. Armageddon is all of a piece with the mark of the beast and 666 and the coming of the End Time. In my own Christian culture it proves only that the devil makes work for idle hands.

'Bloody Jehova's Witness bastards again,' said Peter. 'Why can't they leave people alone? Poor old John would be turning in his grave.'

Beyond a direct personal experience such as these, one could sense the changing tone of the times. If you are young in London now and have eyes in your head, you can see much of the world pass you in the street. It was the same then, and the people who made most impact on my bus rides across the metropolis were the Rastafarians, who often carried sufficient stereo apparatus to make your ears bleed. From their pulsating speakers came one of the soundtracks of the age, Bob Marley's Exodus. To many of all creeds, races and musical tastes, my instinctive feeling towards Bob Marley was sacrilege. I could not bear to listen to a note he played. This was and is an heretical view.

In his defence, the causes for the rise in Rastafarianism were deeply sympathetic. The black populations of the Americas had been as wretchedly exploited as any group in history when their ancestors were stolen from Africa into slavery. Abolition brought scant improvement in the circumstances of millions, and in 1914 the Jamaican Marcus Garvey, leader of the Universal Negro Improvement Association, predicted the 'crowning of a black prince who shall be the redeemer'. In 1930 Prince Ras Tafari was crowned Haile Selassie I of Ethiopia (his name meant 'power of the trinity'), and a religion was born with a living god, Jah.

Rastafarianism viewed whites as inferior to blacks and sought their punishment. It dreamed too of a new kingdom of blacks returned to Africa, ruled over by Jah, a movement of the people. The dramatic dreadlocks were a later affectation. Most white British people had little understanding of Caribbean culture then, beyond the voodoo nonsense in *Live and Let Die*, where Roger Moore moved amongst West Indian stereotypes rolling their eyeballs and slicing the heads off chickens. So, the relatively widespread understanding of Rastas, promoted by Marley and enthusiastically promulgated through music papers like *NME* and *Sounds*, was a positive step in racial understanding.

The problem with Rastafarianism was threefold, in my view. The music, for one. Then, the white Rastas squatting in Brixton after they'd missed the train home to Dorking one night. Above all, the evidently addictive smoking by all concerned of the wisdom weed ganja. I was no prophet, but what this did to the minds of so many was beyond question. It didn't seem a way to oneness to me, more a self-deluded seedbed for losing your place in life's book, and in the worst cases sliding down the slope to harder drugs. This is still a tricky point of view, but people who talk of obtaining some weed from their 'man in Kilburn' make my blood temperature rise. Whatever the sociology of it all, my school friend George started on weed, progressed quickly to heroin, became purveyor to the upper crust of both at our university, and was dead before he graduated.

It seems heavy-handed just to pick on Jehovah and Jah, or to pick on them at all. They had the defence that there was either some wrong-headed exegesis to back them up or a social movement which demanded their creation. However, elsewhere there was a different order of religious behaviour for which it seemed appropriate to use the term evil.

The worst came in 1978 when the Jonestown Christian cult in Guyana committed mass suicide. Jim Jones, a side-burned fake healer and sexual obsessive, ran the People's Temple in Redwood Valley, California. On the brink of exposure as a fraud at his utopian plantation in South America, he killed a congressman and a camera crew and then laced the grape juice of 900 disciples with cyanide, all of whom drank it and died. 276 were children. Jones was precisely the kind of messianic criminal we saw depicted in *A Man Called Ironside*, which was set in the same San Francisco environment and starkly contrasted square Detective Ed Brown and his sidekick, Eve, with the poisonous remaining petals of flower power.

Up and running too by the time I left school was the UFO Doomsday cult, Heaven's Gate, another Californian excrescence looking to catch a lift off Comet Hale-Bopp and fly away to life on a sexless plane above the human level. Thirty-nine ground crew eventually killed themselves, eight of whom had already been castrated in preparation. Meanwhile (and I felt Sri Lankan Charlie would have loved this) the science fiction books of Lafayette Ron Hubbard and his home-brewed mental science of Dianetics united as the Church of Scientology, about which the less said perhaps the better.

The pressure on those of us who wanted to say 'hang on a minute' to devout atheists was becoming unbearable. One of my main areas of study in my last year at Dulwich was History, now taken beyond broad-brush accounts of Romans, Normans and Nazis, and involving original research into eighteenth- and nineteenth-century thought. My first exposure to 'enlightenment' had been hot and Buddhist and had proved positive for the Buddha and those who followed in his measured footsteps. The Enlightenment we studied for A level was the cold philosophical counterpart to geology and biology, doing its level best to destroy the concept of any god, anywhere, at any time. It was nearly ten years since Barry Evans had first unlocked the secrets of the earth and the universe to us in Form JC, and now we sat in History 6B like a gathering of polytechnic junior lecturers, arguing the toss over long-dead debates. Logic was all, passion an impostor.

The names of big intellectual guns were rolled out across the slightly carpeted room with its daring record player in one corner. Thomas Hobbes and John Locke had dissected deism with the scalpel of philosophy and left it in an irrecoverable condition, allowing Thomas Paine to deliver the American Revolution, the French Revolution and the *coup de grâce* for religion in his 1796 Enlightenment text, *The Age of Reason*: 'I do not believe in the creed professed by the Jewish Church, by the Roman Church, by the Greek Church, by the Turkish Church, by the Protestant Church, nor by any church that I know of. My own mind is my own church.'

Attractive words, they inflicted no new doubt on me. Doubt was, and is, always there in everything. But taken with the manifest absurdity of so much which passed for religious life at the end of the twentieth century, they allowed me to wonder whether the best course was simply to cut and run from all religion. I spent New Year's Eve at a party in Forest Hill with my girlfriend as 1979 yielded to 1980. The eighties. What would they be like? When I spoke to her recently for the first time in a while, she reminded me that that was the night I told her, a sweet, tough, attractive and articulate defender of her faith, that God definitely did not exist. In truth I was merely floating an idea in the spirit of testing what we both thought. It certainly wasn't my actual position, and it never occurred to me until this conversation that she might have taken what I said to heart. Apparently it felt like a right uppercut to her spiritual chin. Blasted teenage boys, is there ever a creature so arrogant? I now wish I'd told her what happened little more than a week after I'd wrecked her faith.

Before I could go to university, I had to work for a year to pay for it. I spent most of 1980 employed at Harrods. This was a place of many wonders, an eye-opener for a Bromley boy, but working there was more a matter of stacking or shifting stock than contemplating any dialogue between belief and disbelief at the start of a fresh decade. That was fine by me. They paid my wages, and anyway the temporary enticement of the dark byways of nihilism was soon to seem merely self-indulgent.

Harrods was not the first place I had sought a job. I had worked elsewhere and failed twice already. My first dismissal came at the Waldo Road Refuse Depot in Bromley where a temp agency sold me as a semi-skilled labourer. A new dustcart hangar was under construction and I was left alone with another incompetent called Winston. We were to proof the bottom four feet of some steel girders with a good layer of pitch. Our tools were one stiff brush each and one pot of pitch between two, which we replenished from a barrel. All we had to do with these girders, which lay horizontally in rows raised up from the ground on scaffold, was make sure we painted the correct end. By the end of the day we had painted thirty girders, each and every one at the wrong end. Winston and I were sitting in the Portakabin with two cups of tea congratulating ourselves on a job well done when the foreman's oaths began to flow from the other end of the depot. I believe that under European legislation today it is no longer appropriate to call two honest workers 'a pair of c—ts' before manually evicting them from the workplace, but under the rules of natural justice applying then, he was within his rights.

I was not dismissed from the second job. It merely sapped my will to exist. Beware, young people, of small ads in the *Evening Standard* with no basic wage and On Target Earnings sufficient to buy a Porsche. I mustered at a glamorous office at the top of Southampton Row in Holborn and watched a training presentation for Liberty Life Assurance, an insurance scheme aimed exclusively at women. I was given a clipboard and hundreds of pink leaflets and told to go out into the street to approach potential customers. I could see this job might be fun, but there was a catch. To get paid I had to persuade these women to give me a phone number so that one of the high-pressure sales demons back at HQ could close the deal. At the end of day one I had two numbers at £2 each.

I carried on like this for a few weeks, flirting with the shallows of failure, but was fortunate to be able to confide in a fellow number-harvester called Jan from Poland, who I met for a sandwich most lunchtimes in the open space at Paternoster Square. Jan took twice as many numbers in an hour as I did in a day. He had to. Back in Poland he had a young wife and baby and an uncertain future. He'd come to the attention of the Communist authorities with his translation of George Orwell's

Animal Farm, and was unemployable back home. Jan was amused that an old leftie who'd taught me English initially believed that Orwell was satirising fascism before the penny dropped and he realised that communism was the target. Jan liked this. He loved Britain, but was aware that while we remembered brave Poles in the air force during the war, Poland was stuck with Soviet rule afterwards with direct consequences for him. To him, our left wing was congenitally naïve.

Jan was twenty-eight, and the ten years-difference in our age and the harshness of his life gave him an almost paternal influence on me. One lunchtime I told him of my disillusioned feelings about the Church, religion, the whole shebang, that I couldn't see the point to it any more. His response reminded me of the occasion when I told an accountant friend of Peter's that society ought to abandon money and possessions. Jan put me instantly straight, blue eyes gleaming and words flowing from under his blond moustache.

For him, the Church in Poland, or the honest part at least, connected back to Christ. Christ was a liberator and agent of personal spiritual change, a timeless resistance leader. Jan's parents' souls had been saved by their devotions at church when what they were asked to do in factories was destroying them. Labouring under the Soviet yoke, the Church, to them, was Poland's only salvation.

I was so surprised. I'd presumed that Jan's obvious rebelliousness would automatically be accompanied by anti-establishment Church beliefs. He urged me not to deride belief on the grounds that, if nothing else, you'd never know when you'd really need it. Then he went off to gather more phone numbers and I to tread the hard pavements of London, spiritually refreshed but still useless at the job.

The improbable hero of my new enlightenment became Bamber Gascoigne, an academic best known for his drawling delivery as the chairman of a television quiz for young boffins, *University Challenge*. Gascoigne had been commissioned by Granada Television to make a definitive documentary series called *The Christians*. Thirteen solid hours of it. On ITV! As an occasional producer, I will testify that Bamber would not be asked to do this today. If he were a TV chef cooking his way round the recipes of the Holy Land bumping into *Big Brother* contestants at every shrine, there might be six half-hours in it.

In the seventies his series was serenely unconcerned with the vanity of its presenter, his safari suits or his Fotherington-Thomas delivery. He was learned, educative and occasionally witty, including a nice gag about St Simeon, the first Christian hermit who sat on a pillar of rock high over the Syrian desert, shouting advice to pilgrims below. With minimal lift in his starter-for-ten eyebrows, Bamber wondered if this might have been the very first agony column. I missed a lot of the series when it was first transmitted, but for the first time since *The Water Babies* I owned a book I felt impelled to read and then read again: Bamber's text expanded on his series under the same title with evocative photos by his wife.

I was clearly more of a god botherer than the average teenager, but the gaps in my Christian history were like canyons. All we seemed to know was that a man was crucified and, other than the Crusades, the next point came fifteen hundred years later when Henry VIII became head of a new Church of England. Thereafter I was only slightly more knowledgable than most, and that only because they didn't seem to care. I knew about dissenting Methodists and the work of the Salvation Army because I lived amongst active members, and I had a schoolboy knowledge of the Victorian Gothic Revival in church architecture because I was part of a minority who occasionally went to church.

Bamber's easy and fact-packed prose took me for the first time to the years immediately following the crucifixion, to the conversion and journeys of the apostle Paul, to Peter in Rome. I understood at last the disadvantage Christians have which does not apply in other faiths. Judaism, Hinduism, and Islam are all still practised in the language in which they were originally devised. Christianity passed through Aramaic, Greek, and the Latin of its greatest promoter, the Roman Empire, before it splintered into Spanish or French or English. So many of us shrugged our gormless shoulders when we gave up Latin for German aged twelve, citing received opinion that the former was a dead language and the latter the coming common tongue for international trade. That was a mistake on both counts.

Sometimes a reader finds a question answered that they weren't aware had been on their mind. Betty and Peter had aspirational friends for whom two weeks on a sun-lounger were not sufficient. They returned from holidays with tales of liqueurs drunk and repulsive animal parts eaten, and while our guard was down would chirrup about the simply marvellous Etruscan vases. We weren't sure what this word could possibly mean. Their puzzling trips were the only ones for which we'd have been grateful to see the holiday slides. Another word they mystified us with was Byzantium. I half knew it as an adjectival derivative and bluffed with it in essays about the corn laws, but they seemed to be referring to an actual place they'd been. Why couldn't they go to Majorca like everyone else?

Bamber took me to Byzantium. He told me that the key figure in the international rise of my religion had been a soldier in York, Geoffrey Boycott country, whose father had risen through the ranks to become one of four joint emperors. When he died his son, Constantine, was elected in his place, and on his way back to Rome from England he believed that he saw a sign superimposed on the sun, a monogram of the letter CH and R (the Chi-Rho, first letters of Christ in Greek) and the words '*In hoc signo vinces*' (in this sign shalt thou conquer). He captured Rome on his return and, attributing his good fortune to the sign, he announced that Christianity was now the official language of the Roman world. In order to control this sprawling empire, he built a new capital on the Bosphorus bridging point between Europe and Asia and called it Constantinople. It had previously been called Byzantium.

And Bamber had more. Those of us who were confirmed were promoted up the Christian ladder, away from muttering the mere Lord's Prayer in assembly to the heights of proclaiming something called the Creed in our little Tuesday communions. We were never sure what it was, but now I knew that the Roman Emperor Constantine had insisted it be agreed by a gathering of bishops at Nicaea forty miles west of Constantinople on the Sea of Marmara. There was even a date, 20 May 325. I'd assumed it was written by the Victorians, but we were uttering words written nearly seventeen hundred years before. I felt so connected through time and language to the Christian history that if I'd owned a car I'd have stuck one of those little fish on the back.

Well-produced television can force a programme to focus on the killer detail, and Bamber had plainly refined his research. Each sentence of his book was a nugget, whether teaching me the role Paul played in abandoning circumcision as an entry criterion to Christianity as it was unlikely to lure potential adult converts, or that the dome on the cathedral named after Paul in London wasn't as marvellous as we'd been taught: the dome on Santa Sophia in Constantinople was built one thousand years before Christopher Wren was born.

With Bamber in my rucksack to guide me, I took a break from my labours at Harrods and went with some companions to see some of his promised riches for myself on a student rail pass. The further we penetrated into a hot European summer, rolling by train through villages and towns and cities, the more Bamber's Christian narrative made clear to me that the events which mattered most, which changed lives, were the principled rebellions of good people refusing to submit to spiritual corruption in their Church. The thrust of the Christian story was of a two-thousand-year-old institution which became strong, then lax and narcissistic when it had too much money, and was resurrected when it returned to the simple ways of old. It was a faith which required concentrated focus. It attracted men and women who liked to dress up and play power games, but having achieved the height of their power, they always fell, usually just before a revival, and as they went down they usually took good lives with them at the stake.

The difficulty for me was this. I wasn't sure if I was a committed Christian, but I was sure of my enthusiasm for the phenomenon called Christianity, which at its truest pointed towards simplicity and calmness. Yet, as we passed through the great art galleries of France and Italy all the way to the baroque immensity of the Vatican, the painting and sculpture commissioned by the powerful through time seemed anything but simple. I really couldn't see a living god in the Duomo in Florence, or in the fat faces of Leonardo da Vinci's many takes on Mary and Child. We saw a sun-baked production of a Shakespeare history play in an amphitheatre above Lyon. Even with my poor grasp of French we felt the tensions and dilemmas could apply in the present day. Religious art made at around the same time, on the other hand, left me cold – there was nothing in those faces but self-satisfaction or caricatured martyrdom.

As with my two experiences of enlightenment, one Buddhist and calm, the other Rational and deadly, I was experiencing two renaissances. While my travel companions wrote enthusiastic postcards home describing the treasure trove of European art, I wrestled with understanding the complex history of my country's religion. I was disappointed by the Renaissance promoted and adored by art historians, where dotted lines of gold paint flowed from the Archangel Gabriel's eyes into the womb of the Virgin Mary at the Annunciation. Mine felt more urgent, like a casket of knowledge to which I had been thrown the key.

This did not make me an iconoclast, but I felt more awe sleeping under the stars for the first time in a field by the river Rhone looking up at the universe than I did in any gallery or cathedral. Reading by the light of a little torch a passage about the rise of the Methodists and the forays of John Wesley into the West Country of England, I felt like the conflicted and troublesome William Blake. Today he would be a great multi-media artist and writer. In 1788 he settled for engraving aphorisms into copper plate: 'He who sees the Infinite in all things sees God. He who sees the Ratio only, sees himself only. Therefore God becomes as we are, that we are as he is.'

Blake seemed to have answers to both the zealous atheist and the fundamentalist deist, critical to his time and still crucial to me as I shielded my eyes against the sun. While staring up at the Palace of the Popes in Avignon, I reflected that it was built on the medieval proceeds of selling indulgences, and wondered what was the tipping point in a religion from respectful observance to the vulgar abuse of power. Yet within the precincts of the palace, the glorious sound of a choir and organ shook the afternoon air with music that had once been thought to represent the glory of heaven. Would I wish it never to have been composed, all this alienating art to remain unpainted? Sipping from a bottle of Orangina, I realised I was not qualified to be the judge and that all art and pleasure flow best when tainted by a paradox within.

A Mighty Wind

When I arrived at Exeter University in the autumn of 1980, I was old enough to have an order of priorities in mind. It read something like this.

1. Financial Survival.
2. Penetrating the human mind by studying a degree in Psychology, thereby securing something called a First.
3. To mess about in some kind of theatrical activity.
4. To continue to explore faiths, with special reference to Christianity.
5. To play football for the university team.
6. To be a bit monkish about the opposite sex, careful of distractions.

Many years later I am able to audit the success with which I followed these priorities.

1. It was a financial disaster.
2. I got something called a Third.
3. I became more enmeshed in the theatre than Pinocchio.
4. Let me tell you about Roger the Christian.
5. Never got a game, utterly trumped by lads from the Midlands who'd played every Saturday since they were seven.
6. I'll come back to that one.

Let me speak unto you of Roger the Christian. This is not, as you might first think, the name of an unkind party game. Roger was a man. Roger was also a Christian, and I never really found out how he got on to my case. Was it at the Freshers' Squash where in the first week undergraduates cruised tables manned by enthusiastic society treasurers, dooming them to three years thereafter of potholing or ornithology in place of a social life? Did I dally at the Christian table? I don't think so. Or was it the one occasion I went to a service at the university chapel where I squirmed on my seat with boredom and decided never to return? I don't know.

Roger had a Messiah complex, but that was okay because lots of young men had those. They fell into two categories. The first group wanted to look, sound and be like John Lennon. There were plenty of those; 'Imagine' on the stereo, the shampoo put in their wash bags by their mums unopened. The Lennons' image was quite easy to nurture. Simply buy some round glasses, grow your hair and part it in the middle. The Lennon I knew best, Colin, also drove a VW camper van, and is now something lucrative in the City. Of course he is. How did an ordinary nineteen-year-old have the money to buy and run a new camper van?

The Lennons paid lip-service to a general, unfocused leftishness with an atheist twist. Imagine there's no heaven, it's easy if you try. I liked the Lennons. They were harmless, dreamy, and, at the end of my first term at university, in a state of utter grief after their hero was shot outside the Dakota building on the Upper West Side in New York. Not long afterwards they began to vanish from the face of the Earth. It was as difficult to be a Lennon with 'Woman' being played as your hero's last song as it was when Elvis was commemorated with 'Way Down'. As Colin might say now, the bottom fell out of the Lennon market for some years after that, but he had been the first suburban guru, of that there is no doubt.

The other men with a Messiah complex were like Roger, but here we must identify two subspecies, of which Roger was an unusual blend of both. The first sub-category wanted to look, and be, like some apparently freewheeling hero from popular culture. At that time this could be Shoestring, Doyle from *The Professionals* or Roger Daltrey from The Who. Roger the Christian was unusual in that he was like Daltrey's identical twin, with long, fair, curly locks, baby-blue eyes, cheesecloth shirt, visible groin in tight blue jeans, sandals. But Roger was a crossover into the other subspecies – the University Christians – and this gave him both his gift and his weakness.

The Christians in my hall in the first year were organised like a professional sales team. Their clothing was dreadful by any standards, they all wore the wrong glasses, their hair grew, but not in recognisable styles, and they had the groovy vibe of a deputy bank manager. Yet they were ruthless. The whiff of a rumour that someone was homesick had them knocking on the door with their mobile coffee 'n' biscuit unit. I can't say I ever heard screaming from inside these rooms, but you'd often notice the next morning that the homesick one was surrounded on all sides at breakfast and not left alone until he or she was ready to stir the Nescafé for the next recruit.

Roger the Christian did not really fit in with this lot. His good looks went against him in the view of the dowdy upper echelons of the team. This was his weakness, and, sensing that he was a prophet without honour in his own land, Roger became a one-man hit squad randomly picking on people such as me. In as much as he was not actually an embarrassment to be seen with like the Christian A team, I didn't mind sharing the odd lunch with him. If Roger wanted to talk about 'Jesus Christ Our Saviour' as if He was sitting next to us earwigging our conversation, that was fine so long as I got my sponge pudding and custard.

I'm not sure what Roger was really after from me. Perhaps he had secret instructions to build bridges into the domain of the socially acceptable. One Friday evening he caught me with a mouthful of rhubarb crumble and asked what I was doing the next morning. There could only be one answer to this, which he knew very well already. Nothing. Students never did anything on Saturday mornings.

So Roger said there was a sort of Christian-type thingie in a meeting room in one of the halls of residence and would I go with him? He made it sound a bit like a date, as if he didn't really know all the people there and was worried about turning up alone. I agreed to meet him outside the place at ten the next day.

The large ground-floor meeting room in Hope Hall had windows down both sides and views of the leafy grounds. A dozen rows of seats had been laid with an aisle through the middle. When Roger and I went in it was already nearly full and as quiet as a grave.

'What's all this then, Roger?' I said in the barest whisper.

'Shush,' he urged, before lowering his head, the curls falling down either side of his face creating a personal prayer screen. I sat like the man who doesn't know the words to the National Anthem, the only one not lost in prayer. Looking about me, I saw magazine racks and armchairs piled in one corner. Surely this was a TV lounge for students. How had it become an improvised chapel?

I looked around the room wondering if there were any faces I knew. None, except for the speccy apparatchiks from the Christian Union in my hall, second row from the front. Interestingly, they had superior officers here filling the row in front of them, from which group a young man of postgraduate age stood up and addressed the room. He'd make a good surgeon somewhere now – one of those men on hospital rounds who exert their authority over patient and junior alike by speaking at the volume of a mouse, making all listeners crane in obeisance.

In the faintest murmur he introduced the man who was to lead the next two hours, whose name I never caught. He was an American male in a dark suit. Forty. Bland-looking, well-fed, but not fat. He'd done this before. He invited us to pray.

I was sitting on the end of a row, and when he instructed us to hold hands I gave thanks for not having to link up with anyone to my left. From my right, Roger's hand grasped mine and clutched it. If repeating, 'Oh God, Oh God,' under my breath can be called praying, I suppose I joined in. After two minutes of this agony, the American snapped his head up like a trainer who'd warmed up a sports team, and the gathering shook itself down with little giggles.

With the benefit of hindsight, it seems the American was playing a game of four quarters. In the first quarter he talked to us like normal human beings in the dullest way about world events and the challenges of the student life. At this stage I formed the impression that I had come for a boring little self-help lecture. The second part of his script robbed me of this illusion, because from a standing start he began to tell us that everything wrong with the world, from the Soviet Union to our essay crises, was our fault for not giving up enough prayers to God. God was displeased with every one of us in the room.

No, I didn't believe it either. In 1981, nobody in any church I had entered or encountered would have dreamed of talking to its flock like that, but talk was cheap for this guy. It was full-scale denunciation next.

He began hollering and yelling and screaming about Satan moving among us every minute of every day, and I wondered if these poor Christians had booked the wrong act from a brochure of guest speakers. Surely they felt like me, didn't they? That we should leave the room, fetch the head of the building and have this moron expelled from the campus?

They did not. The only word for the look on their faces was 'rapt'. They knew where he was leading them.

I had to admire his style. He got rhythm. He'd ease up on our wickedness every now and then and bring the room so far down you could hear the excited breathing of his subjects. Then off he'd go, like a sniper checking that every head had taken some of his shot. I slunk down in my seat. He wasn't hitting me.

At the point of maximum emotional battery, he took us into stage three.

'Now, I command you, in the name of the Lord, if you hear voices and strange tongues let them come forth. Heed, hearken to the holy spirit. Oh Lord, speak though us. Let your word be heard.'

I'd heard louder voices on football terraces, but not many. This man could have sold whelks from a stall in a hurricane.

Now he was quite still. There was a silence. From the confident front row, I heard what I took for rather rude conversation. Okay, the chap was an arse, but there was no need to talk over him. The conversation rippled back towards me, row by row, until I was sitting in the middle of an unquiet mob immersed in a Christian practice of which I had never heard. They were 'speaking in tongues'.

What a load of twaddle. I wanted to stand up and tell them to look at themselves. The three girls in the row in front of me were waffling in identifiable fractured Hebrew they'd gleaned on a kibbutz, blended with a bit of O level German and recovered baby language. It could have sounded like they'd had a stroke, but to me there seemed something calculated about it. Before long one of them was giving a good impression of having some kind of orgasm with an '*ah*' and an '*ooh*' and a proper climax, followed not by a cigarette but a small stream of burble as she came down.

Then stage four: oneness. I stiffly avoided Roger's gaze and he had to make do with holding the hand of the bloke on the other side of him. The American gave us a bit more view-of-the-world stuff with a special slant towards Iran and bade us good morning.

Roger followed me out as I walked briskly down the driveway of Hope Hall and back to civilisation. Back at my hall of residence, every good student was still asleep, so we had the common room to ourselves.

'So, Paul, did you enjoy this morning?'

Sometimes you only get one chance at the truth, and this was mine.

'Rog, did you know that was about to happen?'

'What?'

'That man.'

'Not exactly. The other guys do the bookings.'

'Did you know those stupid girls would be coming on their seats?'

'I think that's a bit crude.'

He hadn't heard anything yet.

'Roger, let me be clear here. That was the closest I ever wish to get in my life to the Nuremberg rally. Do you know what subject I'm studying?'

'English.'

'No, Roger, f—ing Psychology, and what you and I have just witnessed was an appalling experiment in mind control. What the f—k was it about? It's not Christianity, for sure.'

Perhaps I've always felt overprotective of our capacity for language. It's so plainly the highway to understanding what makes Man. To see these overgrown children allowing themselves to be manipulated by that crass snake-oil salesman touched a nerve. Roger attempted to placate me with the Christian justification, and spoke of the harvest festival a few weeks after Jesus had ascended into heaven, the Feast of Pentecost. All the disciples, including new recruit Matthias, taking the place of Judas, who had not worked out well, were gathered with other believers when a mighty wind rose around them. They saw what seemed like tongues of fire between them dispensing the Holy Spirit. When they turned to talk to each other, the Mesopotamians, Libyans, Cretans and all, the language barrier between them had dissolved. They seemed to have been blessed by the Holy Spirit with a commonly comprehensible tongue.

'So what about the Tower of Babel, Rog?'

'What about it?'

'That's when God decided all the nations of the world must speak in different tongues. I mean, make your bloody mind up.'

Roger looked hurt.

'It's only the third time I've been, Paul. I wanted to see how you'd react.'

'Look Rog, what you do with your Christianity is your own business, but I just hate charlatans. That man was a con artist.'

'You can't say that.'

'I just have. Seriously, if I could think of anyone I could go and see at this bloody university, I'd shop the lot of you.'

Despite the fact that our hands had been entwined, there was a certain froideur between us after that. As the years went by, I felt badly about this. He really was a loner, and in a way his instincts were ascetic, almost monkish. I doubt that he returned for many more of those meetings himself. What frightened me about them was that if I had not been invited by him as if to a secret club, I'd never have known what these people were up to.

Roger did pop up on my radar occasionally on the campus, and I felt a certain pride that none of my other friends knew anyone like him, while none of his friends would have known anyone like me. Once, when he saw that I was putting on the odd pound, he helpfully explained that the way in which he lost weight was by not eating for a week, a diet plan I was as likely to follow as a life of tongues of fire.

He must have worked hard, for he was awarded a top-of-the-class Biology degree, and a few days before we were due to leave at the end of our third year, he knocked at my door. I asked him in for a cup of tea, but he seemed to be on his rounds – mine was not his only port of call that afternoon. With the solemnity of the young vicar he really should have been, he asked me what my plans were now we'd graduated. I was touched that he should care. I told him and asked him in return.

'I've been praying for guidance on that, Paul. I can't say it's been easy. I have been uncertain what I should do. So yesterday I went to the Job Centre.'

This did not bode well. Young men with crack degrees in sciences usually aimed higher than the Exeter Job Centre.

'And as I looked amongst the advertised jobs, a single word came out from one of them as if in answer to my prayers.'

'That's great, Rog. So what are you going to be?'

'I start work tomorrow at a fish-packing factory on the Marsh Barton Trading Estate.'

'What, sort of a marine biologist role?'

'No, I'm going to be a fish-packer.'

I made a little joke. 'You'll be a fisher of men there, eh, Rog.'
He shimmered with inner peace as I dunked a digestive.
'Precisely.'

I never really understood the university Christian position on
sexuality. The official line was no sex before marriage, but I
suspect one or two flew under the radar by getting engaged. The
problem and the joy of my own romantic life at university was
that it was of a piece with a prevailing ethos of chaos. This was a
curious outcome. I had arrived with such calm resolution and
soon became overstretched. Too many plays, too much responsibility, too much work, too little cash, and after a while too much
romance.

On Sunday mornings I walked tiredly down to Exeter Cathedral and sat through a service, but I was always thinking of the
thousand things I had to do by Monday. One Sunday it was so
busy at the cathedral that my girlfriend and I had to sit in different
rows, and I became aware that one of the most senior members of
the cathedral close was giving her the eye from his pulpit. What
goes wrong with men the minute they put on a costume?

As we approached graduation, I was as optimistic as ever about
our future, while she seemed to be in agonies, making our latter
months something of a struggle. Only decades later did I realise
that she was desperately worried about how we were going to
manage in the real world with jobs in different cities. My strategy
had been to hope for the best rather than the worst. This did not
wash with her, and though she wanted to grow closer, she grew
more distant with every day. I was too busy for paradoxes, but the
greatest irony of all is that she was quietly deepening her own
Christian faith. She just didn't think to mention it to me, even
when we went to see Shere Church in Surrey near her home,
where a fourteenth-century anchoress had herself bricked into a
little room for life to aid her devotions.

In some despair at the end of our final term, we went for a trip
to Cornwall, which did not begin propitiously. Her parents had

just bought her a little Renault to get about the world post-university, but as we prepared to set off for the deep west, she insisted that I drive. I politely refused. This was her car, a present from her family who had worked hard to provide it. It wasn't for me to steal the fun of whizzing down the A30.

As she turned the key in the ignition, she said, 'I've got something to tell you.'

'What?'

'I'm not very good at roundabouts.'

I should have said, 'Never mind, I'm sure you are,' but I actually said, 'Oh, for God's sake, let's just go, shall we.'

As we approached the first roundabout of the journey there was no traffic, and she passed through it without changing gear. At the second there was a coach coming the other way, but she seemed to have mistaken the accelerator for the brake and actually hurtled across its flanks. I winced but held my own counsel. As we neared the third roundabout, there was a steady line of traffic circumambulating like Buddhists round a stupa, and I could see her foot going to the accelerator again.

'No, no, no,' I said, yanking on the handbrake and grabbing the wheel.

We ground to a halt by the kerb and she began to cry, punching me once on the upper arm.

'I told you I couldn't do roundabouts.'

'Well how the f— did you pass your test?'

'I don't know. I think the examiner must have fancied me or something.'

Given that she could draw the attention of a cathedral preacher from thirty yards, this was quite plausible. My next action was inevitable, and I spared her by not speaking my thought, which was, 'I'm too young to die.' I drove.

We crossed Devon and most of Cornwall with hardly a word, and the tension crackled in the Cornish afternoon breeze as we arrived at Marazion opposite St Michael's Mount, the British copy of Mont St Michel off the coast of Brittany. I had found the bed and breakfast in a newspaper, immediately attracted by its cheapness. This proved to be an expensive mistake. When we arrived, we headed to our bedroom to heal our relationship but, before the healing could begin, there was a soft knock at the door.

It was the owner of the B&B. She wanted us to come downstairs for some cocoa. Adjusting my dress, I spoke to her through a crack in the door and said thank you, but no thank you, we were tired after our journey and so forth. I closed the door but could hear no footsteps retreating to the stairs, so I opened the crack again. She was still there. Her husband had warmed the milk, she said, and was putting a few biscuits on a plate too.

I had no alternative but to say we'd be down in a minute. I closed the door to face the unhappy countenance of my partner.

'What did you say that for?'

'They've warmed the milk.'

Five minutes later, one cosy couple and one looking daggers at each other were gathered in the twee sitting room, which I realised had no television. In this intimate sanctum the scales dropped from my eyes. That bloody fish sign was everywhere. These were Christians, and it did not require a mystic to divine that they wished to talk with us about God. The more they probed about us, the more we closed ourselves off from them. We both knew we were at a crisis point which with some thought on our part could yet be overcome, but we equally knew salvation wasn't going to come from this insipid pair over cocoa. We were Christian enough to know that sometimes you must have the humility to ask for help, but we were both proud enough not to want to get it from a pair of wet fish. This was, perhaps, our loss.

Karma Chameleon

The most widely cited use of the maxim 'Stupid is as stupid does' is attributed by Forrest Gump to the wisdom of his late mother. Playing the role of Stupid with some flair, I had lost my girlfriend and my flat and was preparing to embark on a precarious career in a West Country city as a theatre producer. Nemesis awaited.

Any Christian comfort I had taken over the years was beginning to fail me again. The encounter with the B&B couple had been a disaster. It seemed to me that they were of a rising type, who before they'd show real Christian qualities of mercy and grace wanted to exercise control and make judgements. I knew that if I'd gone into the kitchen as the man cooked breakfast (badly, by the way) and said I needed his help, he would not have sought to make me whole again but have broken me into constituent parts first. The only place I felt able to connect with any force beyond present panic was Exeter Cathedral, where I sat and wandered and sat again, not knowing that this was what great cathedrals were designed for, and prayed and thought and tried to take a grip of myself.

So, what did Stupid do next? I had the summer to regroup before going into theatre production, so I tried to find some inner calm. I ran miles at the track in the heat, furlongs on the flat sands at Exmouth beach, and found myself one of those slim little books you feel will give you wisdom. My choice from the shelf was the *Bhagavad Gita*, a seminal and ancient Hindu text written in Sanskrit five hundred years before Christ. I carried it with me wherever I went, sitting with the punks and hippies in Cathedral Green, or in the sand on the beach, and I waited for its wisdom to flower within me. If only I had still known Mr Singh or Oxen they would have spared me the absurdity of this effort. No faith in history is more multifaceted than Hinduism. None requires as much knowledge, acquired if possible in situ, of the pantheon of its gods and their multiple meanings to different castes.

Walking the concrete banks of the River Exe was no match for sitting cross-legged on the Ganges with bodies, petals and perfumes passing by on the water, and the barriers to understanding Hinduism were immense. Mr Singh's Sikhism had been a reform movement, a great act of simplification. Buddhism in principle, was the same, focusing on enlightenment and meditation. Hindus, on the other hand, had many avatars, who were all human manifestations of the preserver of the universe, Vishnu. Krishna was the most popular, though he had many characteristics. He could be charming or prankish or a tender lover, or he could be a warrior and a king. The *Bhagavad Gita* was effectively an extract from the much greater *Mahabharata*, and set out Krishna's beliefs. One minute he was speaking of themes which resonated with me – how to live righteously, to find peace – but the next he was talking of reincarnation and brutal warfare.

The more I read and reread, the more any spiritual truth eluded me, and the stupider I felt. If I were a figure in a Hindu story, I would have been the monkey who grew bored and wanted to live in a different tree, leaving all that was properly learned and precious behind him on an old branch which, now that the clouds had settled in low, he could no longer see or reach.

It was nobody's fault that I'd chosen to teach myself Hinduism from the wrong book in the wrong country at the wrong time, but there were consequences. I felt as if I was losing control of events, which at least showed that I hadn't lost my judgement, because I was.

It was becoming clear that there were great similarities between churches and theatres – the learned behaviour, the feeling that in a congregation or an audience the whole is greater than the sum of its parts. They feel very different, however, when you are standing on a stage alone in an empty theatre or at a mixing desk halfway back into the auditorium. Perhaps it is to do with the acoustic design, but at such times there is a sense of perfect peace in the present moment. If someone walks towards you and contact is made, it can feel as if you are insulated from consequences elsewhere. There is a pact of complicity, but given the nature of young performers and producers it has at its heart a kernel of desire let off the leash. This does not occur in any church I have sat in on my own, which is just as well.

Soon enough it was early autumn and a cast had assembled for our first production. I took my business partner to one side and told him in stern terms that he was not to dabble with any of the actresses. He was crestfallen, but he appreciated my mature good sense and youthful professionalism. Two weeks later I was going out with the leading lady. This gives me the opportunity to note the word that the Greeks first gave to actors who pretended to be things other than what they were for a living – Hypocrite.

There's a lot of hubris in a pair of twentysomethings who believe they have some kind of Antony and Cleopatra thing going on in a house by the Nilus' slime of the muddy Exe estuary, but if Shakespeare hadn't recognised this syndrome as a recurring aspect of romantic affairs he wouldn't have been able to write about it. This gave me two problems. First, if you are going around thinking you are A&C, you are also aware of the ending, which means both of their deaths. The candle must burn down. The second problem was that someone brought me up short near the beginning of it all with a cold slap of Christian reality, and I carried on regardless.

His name was James, a kind, good-hearted lighting designer who seemed at first to think of me with some respect. Many workplaces, most productions, have such a person, like a cat who has its favourites and seems to bring good luck, who is grateful for his home. The reality was that my Cleo was engaged to somebody else. I'd like to say it sounds worse than it was, but of course any excuse makes things seem blacker. He had just moved to Australia on what seemed like a permanent basis, but there were plans for her to join him there eventually. She did take a fair share in the initial approach; but I didn't have to respond. It was an extraordinarily magical time, but I already knew magic was an illusion.

James knew how to twist the knife. In his mild Scottish accent he said, 'Paul, have you not heard of doing unto others as you would have them do unto you?' He didn't say 'Matthew, chapter 7, verse 12', but he and I both knew it was from the Sermon on the Mount, and that if it ever applied to my life it applied right here and now.

That hit home, so far up to the hilt that I nearly didn't spend the night with Cleopatra, but of course I did. I told my business partner what had been said the next day, and he said the man was a silly busybody. He wasn't, though. He was as clear a signpost as I have ever seen, reading 'Stop. Stop and apologise and make good.' I crashed the lights, and a while later everything crashed. A fortune-teller's cart which had been ever present in our affair vanished from its field by the Exe one afternoon and seemed to take our luck with it, like a change of wind in a Thomas Hardy novel. We had both lacked the strength to stop, and though she broke her engagement the origin of the affair seemed to deny it a future. Another bloody paradox, though this one could undeniably be explained, in part, by being based in an untruth.

I retreated to London with my wounds, and one wet day I took the bus up the Edgware Road through Kilburn and Cricklewood to glorious Neasden. And it was glorious. There was more to Hinduism in Britain than going solo with a Penguin edition of the *Bhagavad Gita*. Newly opened in one of the least glamorous suburbs of London was the biggest Hindu temple outside of India, its steps busy with families gathering and getting ready to enter.

I could have gone in, and I badly wanted to. I would have removed my shoes and mixed in and shown all due respect, but I was fearful that if I went into a church and prayed to make things right, there might be a voice there for me, if only from my own saner earlier self. I wondered if, inside this temple, I would see some facet of a conceited minor god of folly which I would recognise as a carved stone version of me.

I walked away.

There was worse to come.

The Missing Finger

I had arrived back in London after university in bad shape, unknowingly heading for my next disaster. Since the backdrop to this involved writing a play about Freud's last days in Vienna before fleeing the Nazis, this may be the moment to lift a few repressions. Many would say I had a broken heart, but I'm cautious about a term properly owned by the grieving. What I will say is that for about a month waking up was a tangible struggle to banish the darkness and desolation.

I paid the usual solitary visits to churches and tried to pray my way out of my despair. This relieved the symptoms if not the disease. One evening I went out for a drink with Matthew, who'd been there with me in JC when Mr Evans predicted the end of the universe. Matt wouldn't be the Samaritans' first recruit for its phone lines, but I hoped if I could just share a bit of the agony it might help. My experience of studying psychology had shown me that, while I was esoterically obsessed with the history of psychoanalysis and its relationship to art and literature, those graduates attuned to obtaining a good degree had written essays about 'coping strategies'. These involved an acceptance that your car really has crashed and somehow you've got to find a way out of the vehicle.

We met at Matt's new workplace near Regent's Park and entered the first pub we found. I bought the drinks, took a breath, and was about to tell him the whole story of Antony and Cleopatra by the River Exe when he went into his own impersonation of the persecuted Job. He too had just split from his girlfriend, and I was treated to his why-me tirade until closing time. If moaning was an Olympic event, Matt won all the medals that night.

Like most of my generation, I'd loved the writing of J.R.R. Tolkien as a child, though I wasn't a reader much beyond that. One chapter in *The Hobbit* was titled 'Out of the Frying Pan and Into the Fire', and the moment was approaching when I'd understand precisely what that meant. Provided with a job in a brass rubbing centre in the basement of St James's Church on Piccadilly by relatives of my university ex-girlfriend, I thanked her by almost immediately beginning a relationship with a young woman working there.

This vicissitude accounted for the next three years of my life. Through her having left a jumper at a rehearsal room in the Arts Theatre off Leicester Square, I became involved, six months later, in writing a play to be performed at this historically loss-making venue (the one about Freud) as well as performing for the last time on stage. There was an interesting psychology in that too. On the first night, despite the fact that I had written it, I could not remember my own lines.

Of course I don't believe in the idea of meddling gods, malign relatives of my fairies at the bottom of the garden. You're given free will and sometimes you get strange luck to go with it. The ideal next girlfriend, as profiled by a therapist for me after the Exeter debacle, would have been a year or two older, of independent means, sound in mind, and with a life of positive educational experiences behind her. The djinns led me to her very opposite, a Catholic actress and wounded product of an English convent education.

In 1890 a brave woman called Miss J.M. Povey wrote a book about her escape from convent life as a Benedictine nun, where she had been called Sister Mary Agnes. The Sister's life had been dominated by a Father Ignatius, who had recruited her aged fifteen:

> I was led by Ignatius to believe that . . . by leaving home and relations I was but obeying the command of Christ to 'leave all and follow Him'. Was there ever such an absurdity as this? I was

not called upon to go on a mission to the teeming millions living in heathen darkness . . . but positively to make myself a prisoner in one particular house . . . I was taught that I could bless and be made a blessing to others, by 'telling the beads', 'invoking the saints', 'confessing sins to man', by 'hearing mass' and by 'reciting various offices'. What incredible folly. I find how great was my delusion, and I do heartily trust that my experience of this folly may be the means of saving girls and boys, men and women, from wasting so much precious and God-given time which it was my sad lot to lose.

This kind of confessional and revelatory account has more than one face. It was very bold for its time but read today, when everyone knows there have been hidden problems in cloistered life, it can also play to anti-Catholic prejudices. My reason for citing this passage is that the book's title is *Nunnery Life in the Church of England*. The misuse of religious power in convents was never merely a matter for Catholics, though many would have us believe otherwise with talk of Papistry. Father Ignatius was operating out of the Church of England, where he was faking miracles – claiming he had brought a woman back to life, and that the infant Jesus in his nativity scene had sat up and smiled at him – and running an order where orphan children in its care were stripped and flogged for whispering in chapel. Penance was the cruellest word in Miss Povey's short but devastating account of a convent on the C of E's watch.

It would be an ignorant Westerner, sneering at the rise of fundamentalism in other regions of the world today, who didn't accept that the Christian establishment wrote the book on this subject. Father Ignatius was allowed the powerful freedom of the pulpit in some of the great churches in the City of London, on Lombard Street and Bishopsgate. He recruited through public meetings in a hall in Bloomsbury. Just as the early Christians took over well-established pagan festivals and made them their own, so heavy recruiting groups like the Jehova's Witnesses will have learned much of their technique at the knee of Christians like Ignatius.

However, my new girlfriend suffered an experience which was the undeniable responsibility of one branch of the Catholic hierarchy, the rider here being an acknowledgement that many convent girls had wonderful childhoods and went on to blameless lives. Like hundreds of thousands of others, my girlfriend was educated at a Catholic convent by nuns, and, while she wasn't flogged, the mental scars were plain to see. When I met her she was the classic rebel from a repressive system, and young men like me were the forbidden fruit, for which young men like me showed their gratitude. Soon enough the tears in the fabric became painfully clear.

The sternly imposed daily devotions had vanished after her schooldays, and if ever there is a person left with a God-shaped hole it is the Catholic convent girl. As the early months of our relationship unfolded, I realised that she believed she had a spirit guide who, if she sat naked, channelling its words through her pen, could give her wisdom and, ultimately, communication with 'the other side'. She was also partial to an occasional evening with the Ouija board. For a while, she thought that Elvis slept at the bottom of our bed. It almost goes without saying that practically every course of action she took was the occasion of guilt. The arrogance of those who told me she was mad came from their self-regard and want of any empathy. She wasn't mad; she was still processing events which had begun a decade and a half before.

We stayed together because we were in love, but we had rows which made *Who's Afraid of Virginia Woolf?* seem like tea with the vicar. If we set off on a journey by public transport, I was never sure we'd end up in the same place, so regularly did she storm off down escalators or fling herself on the wrong train. Eventually we heard that her convent was closing down and that all the nuns were going to a seaside boarding house, so we drove down to look at the empty building in Sussex.

Here was the wall through which she heard two sisters having sex in a bath. There was the statue of Our Lady to whom this little girl had prayed so devoutly for so long. Along the corridor was the classroom where the nuns achieved some of the worst academic results in the country. If you'd been with me that afternoon, you would have protested, as I did some years later, against the new-found zeal of a Catholic Education Secretary and a nearly Catholic Prime Minister for creating more 'faith' schools. I love faiths, but they make poor foundations for open and accountable education. Like wine and cheese and weather and home-grown films, the French, in their insistence on a secular education system, have Dieu on their side.

I sincerely don't mean to complain of my lot, but over the next few years my girlfriend tried to shape me into the thing she needed. She wanted to find my boundaries. I think she was trying to work out what the truth might be through another human being. In many ways I felt like the producer of a one-woman show on a very long run, and though I was prepared to give her help where it was needed, I was not prepared to sign up for the Arthur Miller role with Marilyn Monroe, which was where it was heading.

Many years later she told me she was training to communicate with the spirits, and I wished her good luck with that. She'd found a black and white photograph of a Victorian relative who looked startlingly like her, and she suggested to me that she was the new vessel of the same soul, a kind of reincarnation. Professor Dawkins might have tossed his hair angrily at this and explained that the similarity was more a matter of genes, but I have to admit there really was something in the woman's look, and besides, who was I to spoil a sentiment which gave her happiness?

What did for us in the end was that I couldn't bear another moment of self-obsession. In this particular Catholic girl, her ego had been so crushed by her convent childhood that when it began to restore itself it knew no sating. I could understand this, but I lost patience with the self-centredness of it, not least because through the Freud play I had met a man to whom far, far worse had happened.

It is well known that railway termini, churches and public libraries attract men and women who are unsure where they belong in a harsh society. Some are itinerants, some are ordinary lost souls looking for a sense of belonging. Theatre bars attract a subspecies of this type, who can develop a monomaniacal obsession with an individual play or show. Our Freud play had one. His name was Behrmann.

Mr Behrmann was a small, plump, round-faced man in his late sixties, with something of a Peter Lorre about him. He wore brown or dark green garments with the trimmings of central Europe. I liked him, but there were those in the theatre who hated him. Foremost amongst these was the box office manageress. They were both Jewish, but beyond that there was no common ground. She was a tough, sparky optimist from the box office old school; not an underpaid student on a ticket line, but someone who saw herself as the plucky outward face of a play, any play, even ours, which in truth was not a landmark in British theatre.

She hated Behrmann because he was another kind of Jew. He told stories of concentration camps, of escaped Nazi commandants living in London whose names he knew. He disgusted her by showing the scar where he said the finger had been cut from his right hand.

During performances I could always see him in the front stalls as I went about being unkind to Sigmund Freud. Night after night he hung around after the show and complained that I was still wearing the wrong kind of leather coat for a real Gestapo officer. Yet he was transfixed by us. He wanted to tell us more about what it had been like in a camp, to have us listen to his tales of writing to Mrs Thatcher with the names of the guilty men. He seemed to have a complete knowledge of Nazi persecution of the Jews in the Baltic states from where he came, particularly in

Latvia. This was a part of Holocaust history of which we were terribly ignorant.

The box office manageress loathed me giving him my time.

'I'm afraid you'll have to learn, Paul, that you shouldn't entertain these people. He's raving mad. You shouldn't encourage him.'

I told her that he claimed to have been in Belsen, and she shocked me deeply with her response.

'You don't want to trust a word he says. Some of these sickos get their kicks trying to impress people like that. He's just a liar. I know the type.'

The next evening Mr Behrmann was there as usual and I steered the subject away from his obsession with Nazis to ask something about his present life. His reply seemed to bear her out in every way. In his high-pitched whine of a voice, he said he had been an actor, but there weren't the parts for him now. Stretching credulity he said that he'd starred in films with Frank Sinatra, that he had known all of Hollywood, and as I gazed into his fat little face I realised that she had a point. Behrmann was a fantasist who'd probably lost his finger in the lawnmower.

When the run ended, I didn't say goodbye to him. There was a fire in the theatre and our last night never took place. With the play over, the failure hit home and a dose of pneumonia laid me low for a month. One afternoon I sat, breathing wheezily, watching an afternoon movie called *The Naked Runner*, one of a run of duds starring Frank Sinatra, who'd struggled in the sixties to find a decent film role. A paranoid thriller typical of the time, it would be wholly unmemorable for me had I not heard a high-pitched whining voice coming out of the television from the mouth of a man looking very like Peter Lorre.

I pressed my nose to the screen and almost fell backwards when the actor's hand came into frame. There was the missing finger. Mr Behrmann. I sat through the rest just to check the credits, and there was his name. It had seemed almost impossible that he had been telling the truth about being an actor, let alone one who'd played opposite Sinatra. So had he been telling the truth about everything else all along?

I felt honour-bound somehow to contact him, to say I'd seen him in a film. Other than by me, he had been treated like an unwelcome stray during our run, and that was wrong. But nobody knew how to find him.

As the years passed I still felt bad about him. It had been a confusing time. Why had the box office manageress shunned him? What compelled him to watch my undistinguished portrayal of a Gestapo officer every night? Who had he lost?

Three years later I was on a Routemaster heading out of the City on Cheapside when I saw an old man tottering along the road on the point of collapse. It was Behrmann. I jumped off at the next lights and ran back to him. He was severely diabetic and I sat him down on a bench and bought him a Coke. He sipped it slowly then looked up into my face. He recognised me but he couldn't remember from where. Gently I reminded him.

'Yes, I remember,' he said. 'That awful play.'

At first this impolite assessment of my early work seemed markedly ungrateful from a fattie swigging my Coke, though anyone who'd read the *Daily Mail* review would not have been surprised. As he spoke more, I realised he was not saying how poor the play was, but that it had been awful for him to watch a leather-coated Gestapo officer brought to uncertain life in front of him every night. He had been compelled to watch.

I was due to meet my girlfriend for our daily row on the Strand, and I helped him on to another bus. We sat like two children on the long bench seat at the back where I used to study Mr Singh's badges. I told him that I had seen him in the Sinatra film and he was pleased. Suddenly his senses cleared. He was nobody's fool.

People used to call him a liar for his talking about that film, he said. They didn't like hearing the things he had to say. He caught my eye. We both knew the subtext. Slowly and deliberately he pulled the sleeve of his jacket up above his wrist. A number was tattooed into his skin.

'I have never lied.'

He patted his scuffed and bulging briefcase.

'I've had meetings with some associates today,' he said. 'You just make sure you read the newspapers. I have done something today which they will not reverse.'

It was plain he'd worked himself up into a state for these meetings, which had left him exhausted and stumbling towards the West End alone. At the Aldwych he stood up and, with a formal handshake of thanks, said goodbye. I did watch out for the newspapers, newly alert to old atrocities in the Baltic states just as I had once passionately followed the civil war in Sri Lanka, and a year later a meeting was called in a room at the Houses of Parliament, where the ex-Home Secretary Merlyn Rees was appointed chairman of a committee to look into war crimes committed by men who had escaped to Britain and were still living amongst us.

I had a desk job at the *Independent* at the time, and used my press pass to get in. There in the front row was Mr Behrmann, clutching the committee's mission brief bound in vanilla paper bearing the House of Commons crest. I watched his face as Merlyn Rees set out his clear intent to see that justice was done at last. On screen Behrmann had the demeanour of a fat villain; here he was a plump child with notable courage.

Afterwards I spoke to him in the corridor and told him I had watched out, just as he said. He seemed pleased, though more for me than for himself. To him I was an ignorant gentile who knew nothing of the greatest cruelty in the world. I asked him the question which I had found impossible to answer. Why had the box office manageress done so much to do him down?

'Because she is a Jew,' he replied.

'But you're a Jew.'

'I haven't been a Jew since all this,' he said, patting the parliamentary document.

I needed to be back at work, and I left him sitting on a stone bench, beginning to read through his paperwork. This was to be his Torah from now on. His prayers and curses had been heard; his prophecies at last beginning to come true.

Mapless in Gaza

On the day my wife and I met, we were first alone together in an empty nineteenth-century theatre in Cherbourg. In its first-floor reception room, where a long glass window overlooked the main square, the Mayor of Cherbourg's civic reception for a dozen writers and journalists from London was in full swing. Usually I'd have deployed my stilted French to build bridges between the immaculately dressed locals and the ill-mannered scruffs from across La Manche, but there was this young woman, with whom I escaped through a brown wooden door with gold-leaf edging to a private box looking over an unlit stage.

In that empty theatre, with its stucco heads of great French philosophers and tatty curtains, we sensed a future. A few days later, the two of us properly alone at last in deep Normandy, we stood in another silent place, the main church at Coutances, sheltering from the mid-June heat precisely two hundred years after the storming of the Bastille in 1789. My intended wife, half-American, was in part a product of the revolutionary atheist wave which followed. She sat in the church without a belief. The only thing I couldn't believe was my luck, but I knew she was feeling as I did, that possibility would become certainty in a place such as this before long.

It had been implicit that we would get married from the first few days, but we wanted to become engaged first. On our return we went on a long walk around Regent's Park, coming in at the gate by the large mosque, and by the time we'd reached Baker Street we'd decided to take this next step in Israel. Our reasons for going there were different. She was an intrepid and almost compulsive explorer of new experiences. I was hungry for the richness of its religious associations. I wanted to bring us close to some source of holy spirit, imagined or real. Unknowingly we were about to come closer to the story of Islam.

The British have long had an epic ignorance about the Muslim world. My understanding began badly with a novelisation of a *Dr Who* series, in which he'd travelled back in time to meet Saladin, who was depicted as a black-bearded, gold-toothed stereotype of throat-cutting Arab ruthlessness and not the merciful opponent of Richard I during the Crusades, who spared the lives of Christians when he recaptured Jerusalem in 1187. E.M. Forster was a better literary servant to this great civilisation when I was a little older, and I felt very Mrs Moore when I read *Passage to India* for the first time, the Muslim Dr Aziz a wholly sympathetic character, filled with curiosity and a sad, eventual sense of injustice.

How little we connected. What percentage of the British population knew that when it went for an 'Indian' it was going for a Pakistani or a Bangladeshi, that the thousands of curry restaurants revolutionising its cuisine were run by Muslims not Hindus? A compulsive wanderer into the faiths of others, I'd visited the London mosques in Regent's Park and Whitechapel, and the only aspect I understood was washing my feet. The language was Arabic, and though I'm sure the faithful didn't mean to alienate the curious, that was the effect. I so wanted to kneel down in prayer with the ranks of the observant, but, without any understanding of what I was doing, I'd have looked like I was trying to find a contact lens.

The major problem for the British perception of Islam was in the implications of the word itself and the call it makes upon its own. A Jew has an ethnic identity which leads him to his religion, or away from it. A Christian can make choices along the way to deepen his commitment through rites of passage. A Hindu does not call his religion Hinduism, but Sanatana Dharma, meaning eternal teaching or eternal law. Buddhism takes its name from Buddha, literally the Enlightened One, but beyond the Theravada form in Sri Lanka and Thailand it has many incarnations, from the intensely meditative and focused Zen, with its karate and tightly designed gardens, to the Mahayana of eastern Asia, where Siddhartha Gautama was the first of many Buddhas, with more, yet to come.

Victorian accounts of followers of Mohammed didn't look for any other word than 'Mohammedan', but it was not as simple as they thought. Within a few years of his death, his flock had split into two – the group representing the majority of Muslims today, the Sunni, followers of Mohammed's father-in-law Abu Bakr; and the Shia, followers of Ali, who had been both cousin and son-in-law to the Prophet. From both groups a hundred years later emerged the Sufis, who believed they came closer to God through chant and dance. The Whirling Dervish contingent of the Sufis make your head spin; theirs too. But Sufis also had a reputation for compensating for the early success of Islam by asceticism. The *suf* means the coarse wool they chose to wear. One of the most famous early Sufis was al-Hallaj. He was an ardent admirer of Jesus, and for his pains they crucified him.

This split has parallels in every other faith. But the word 'Islam' literally means 'Obedience' – to the will of God, or Allah. Followers of Islam are called Muslims, or Obedient Ones. Almost no non-Muslim in Britain knew or understood this until very recent times. And Islam knows no international borders. The Umma is the whole-world community of Muslims. Cut one and the rest bleed.

That is why the West began to panic with the Iranian revolution in 1979. Nobody in Acacia Avenue or East 48th Street wanted to tune in to a party political broadcast featuring Ayatollah Khomeini: the rising tide of fundamentalism could hardly have been more counterproductive. At a time when millions internationally had real and committed concerns about the conduct of Israel towards the Palestinians, this new wave guaranteed American support to shore up this awkward new state in its unreformed condition for the foreseeable future.

Somehow the true message of Islam was not coming through. How many knew that Abraham was the first prophet in Judaism, Christianity and Islam? That Mohammed first spoke to God through the angel Gabriel, or *Jibril*. Why hadn't we learned that the stories of Moses, David and even Jesus run through Muslim tradition too? When we set off for Israel I went seeking the landscape of Christ, but what I discovered was the Jewish world which produced him and the progression of thought into Islam which came after him.

That Israel has a lot of history is an absurdly obvious state-ment. If you can drive a car through Jericho, Massada, Shiloh, Beersheba and even Armageddon in a morning you feel the weight of time with every mile on the clock. Less known, and incredibly stupid, is that the hire car motorist in his tiny Opel didn't have the benefit of a map of the country. Unable to agree where the West Bank was occupied or which bit of Jerusalem was the predomi-nantly Arab East, the authorities had responded by refusing to engage with cartography at all.

At first this was not a problem. We flew in to Eilat on the Gulf of Aqaba and headed north through decidedly Israeli terrain, our first vehicle similar to the one my Action Man used to cruise about in. The Israelis had a real talent for making the most of unpromising material. The closed mines at Timna were attributed to King Solomon, but I've seen more impressive operations in Cornwall. The irrigated parts of the Negev desert were claimed to be a Zionist triumph, making a moonscape habitable for the first time, but this overlooked the many Bedouin we met and took tea with in their tents, the world's most hospitable people, who had lived here for millennia.

We stayed by the Dead Sea on the Ein Gedi kibbutz – well-watered, filled with happy faces, like a slice of California. Watching a basketball game there we could have been in Santa Monica. This was an ideal community, the communal kibbutz par excellence, and it was built around two springs. The first gave the place its name; it means Goat's Spring in Hebrew. The second spring spouted millions of American dollars to support it. There was always going to be trouble in this unsustainable paradise.

Finding Jerusalem without a map was easy. Just keep going until the Dead Sea is no longer on your right and turn left at a strange junction. To the south of there was a bullet-ridden ghost town lost by the Palestinians after the Six Day War in 1967. The Israelis had built a water park on its edge, and you entered through this desolate place as if it was included in the ticket price, like part of a Universal Studios tour through a generic set for a shot-up Arab village.

When we reached Jerusalem, the first intifada, a peaceful labour strike by Palestinians, was at its height, but it was doing the tourist shekel no harm. Cluelessly staying in the welcoming Arab part of the city, we roamed without fear all hours of day and night, though what we discovered in the old walled city seemed more peculiar with every visit. Each of the Abrahamic faiths had holy sites in Jerusalem which were the cause of constant battling. There are so many, but for the Jews the main flashpoint is the Wailing Wall, which they believe is the remaining flank wall of the Second Temple destroyed by the Romans. We left the lines of nodding Hassidics there and walked up some steps to the Dome of the Rock, a mosque built around the rock from which Mohammed is said to have ascended to heaven on a staircase of light carrying him back to Mecca. Beneath the rock, hairs from his beard are kept in a shrine, and the Muslims are paranoid that the Israelis are tunnelling underneath.

A couple of stones' throw west again, and the Church of the Holy Sepulchre has been precision-placed over the triple attractions of Christ's crucifixion, his burial and his resurrection. They really don't do maps. It was an unholy mess and the centre of a centuries-old feud over which Christian sect owned it. Five communities – the Latins, Greek Orthodox, Armenian Orthodox, Syrian Copts and Abyssinians – all laid claim, and as we emerged blinking from its gloomy innards to the November sunshine, I felt that the real Jesus would have shut the place down overnight.

At Easter, a Greek Orthodox priest secretes himself in that part of the Holy Sepulchre assigned to Christ's tomb, and all lighting in the church is extinguished. He emerges a few moments later with a blazing torch ignited by a miracle, and all gathered inside climb over each other to light their own candles from the sacred flame. Father Christmas and the tooth fairy are essentially benevolent acts of complicity between a parent and its child, but I'm not so sure about this unholy scrum over a flickering light.

The next morning I looked at the only map to hand of the Holy Land, the one in my King James Bible, and reckoned we could drive down to Bethlehem in a pleasant three-quarters of an hour. As we went south in light rain, the beautiful fringes of the hills of Judea gave way to something a bit flatter, and we were interested to note that both sides of the road looked peculiarly built-up. More than that, all the houses and flats seemed to be set behind an enormous wire fence, and there were numbers of youths standing on their roofs watching the road.

I had just finished the word 'camp' in 'Christ, this is a Palestinian refugee camp' when the first rock hit the car, but by some happy chance it rebounded off the wiper blade squeaking across the front window. I take pride in my flight or fight instinct, and, realising in a millisecond that our hired Opel had Israeli plates and that we had just entered a place where traditional Arab codes of hospitality did not really apply, I slammed my foot on to the accelerator and took off down the dusty road like a runaway train. I was not going to brake, whatever happened. I wouldn't have run over a Palestinian, but his goat would have been a necessary sacrifice.

After five miles of hurtling through the Holy Land the fence finally disappeared and we arrived in the little town of Bethlehem; how still we see thee lie. I got out of the car, my back chilling instantly as the cool breeze hit my sweat-soaked shirt. Much as one might salute aspects of the Israeli way of life, this failure to provide maps to pilgrims could have proved fatal. Much as I sympathised with the plight of the displaced, incarcerated Palestinians, I felt their tactics lacked intelligence when it came to stoning potential supporters from around the world.

The Palestinians had the last laugh, which is the least they deserved. The Church of St Catherine may have marked the spot of Christ's birth, but for us, despite our flight from unholy terrors, there would be no room at the inn. Owing to the intifada, this nativity scene was closed.

In all the strange magic of Jerusalem, I had forgotten that my future wife had come with me on this trip in the expectation that her future husband was going to propose. Back at the hotel later that evening, after a massive detour out of the West Bank and back into Jerusalem via Tel Aviv, I put my plan into operation.

The next morning, checking first with the concierge that I was not going to drive through North Vietnam by mistake, I drove our car under the grand awning of the American Colony Hotel and swept my soon-to-be-intended out of Jerusalem towards the Sea of Galilee. The artists of my childhood Bible must have visited here before they'd rendered their scenes, because the views we saw along the Jordan valley were identical to those in my imagination. It was as if I'd been there before. At Tiberias we stopped at the hot mineral springs which had a reputation for aiding female fertility. We should have paid more attention to that. Then we took a rowing boat out on to the Sea of Galilee and made weak jokes about walking on water.

We had dinner that night at our hotel in Capernaum, at the north end of the great lake, eating St Peter's fish, a phenomenally ugly species with odd finger-like marks by its gills left when St Peter picked up one of its ancestors. The lake's most famous produce, our cheeky Palestinian waiter told us, was actually reared in a pond at a local kibbutz.

Half an hour before dawn the next day I was ready to complete my mission. Driving out of Capernaum north-eastwards. I saw the hill I was looking for sloping up from the lake; the sun was just beginning to rise behind it. I stopped the car, and we walked up the incline until we turned to see all of Galilee below, illuminated by the red and orange first light of day.

That was when and where I proposed to my wife, at dawn on the Mount of Beatitudes, where Jesus had delivered his Sermon on the Mount, as close as I could imagine in the world to a spot where something good and sound and lasting was once said.

She didn't hear me, unfortunately, and true to her social origins she said 'What?' rather than 'Pardon', so I had to say it again. As she considered her reply, I realised that the flat, concrete patch of ground on which I'd solemnly declared myself was a gun turret. She didn't seem to mind, because she gave me a yes.

The sun was climbing ever higher, and to the east we saw an even more imposing range of hills. We jumped into the car and chased the dawn towards them. The view below grew more beautiful with each mile, but as we reached the plateau at the top of the range we noticed that on either side of the road lay the carcasses of dead tanks, dozens of them. Driving on, we saw that the ground was peppered with deep craters too, and before long two fighter jets skimmed low above our head.

I did not need a map to tell me that this time I had brought my new fiancée to the summit of the Golan Heights, where the view encompassed the serenity of Galilee as well as the disputed Syrian and Lebanese borders. There are more dangerous spots for a morning spin in a hired car, but not many. Familiar with the accelerator, I performed a one-point turn and roared down the Heights back to Capernaum, passing the point where we had just become engaged without a second glance.

It was very sad to first encounter a major Muslim community in a place like Israel, where it has existed with a dreadful loss of face for many decades. Back in Jerusalem, we walked through the souk in the Muslim Quarter of the Old City and could see a twofold betrayal of promises as apparent as the scars from a lash.

After World War I, T. E. Lawrence had hoped to secure Western support for a united Arab nation under King Faisal, but instead the Gulf was carved up between the French and the British. Oil, of course. After World War II, the Zionists fought hard to make the British honour Balfour's Declaration that the Jews, now the most persecuted race in history, should be allowed to make a homeland in Palestine; but there was never a point in this process where the question of what the Palestinians might think was answered. They were perceived as wandering Arabs who could make a home anywhere.

They are still there, and their plight makes a tragic spectacle. Imagine how it might feel to enter Canterbury cathedral through a belligerent line of heavily armed French troops backdating a claim to the land because of the Norman Conquests. That is how Muslims feel as they press their way through Israeli lines to the Dome of the Rock.

It is tragic for Islam that Muslims have been presented in recent years mostly in this role as victim, because there are many other tales of Islam's extraordinary and historic greatness. William Dalrymple has made it his life's work to illuminate the accomplishments of the Mughal states in what became India, telling how many British ex-pats drifted away from their strict eighteenth- and nineteenth-century Christianity and converted to Islam, not just because it was politic but as trailblazers for the many Westerners who a century or two later found new faith in the East to replace their moribund belief in the West.

We discovered on our honeymoon that it was not necessary to change continent to find evidence of an historically great Islamic nation; that Spain, country of Franco, Real Madrid and Flamenco guitar had been entirely dominated from the eighth to the fifteenth centuries by the Muslim conquest from the east. Indeed, this had been widely welcomed by thousands who were tired of the yoke of Church and State and converted immediately. Such was the melting together of ideas that the Bible was soon translated into Arabic. Scholars from Britain and elsewhere came into contact with Islamic concepts in philosophy, mathematics, astronomy and medicine entirely new to them, to the great benefit of its relatively new universities.

This is where I had my second encounter with Islam, and, as with many experiences of British life, it began in the historical shadow of one of our own fearful religious wars. We married not far from Wardour Castle, near the border of Dorset and Wiltshire, a classic edifice of battlements and moat which would have looked even more picturesque if it had not been blown to smithereens by Cromwell's forces in the Civil War, the owner being a recalcitrant Catholic. Fortunately, religious affairs had moved on since then, though there were still hoops through which we had to jump. In order to marry in a church you must still have banns read over a period of weeks declaring your intent and inviting the congregation to object. It's an anxious moment when the vicar says, 'And now, this is for the last time of asking,' and you wonder if a voice is about to pipe up from the pews; but we should have relaxed. The vicar told us afterwards he would have been a Buddhist if he had his time again, and advised us to watch out for the organist's extraordinary habit of going off with either the fiancées or the wives involved in weddings. It was a broad Church.

We married a few years before *Four Weddings and a Funeral*, but Richard Curtis had it about right. Part of my story that day was getting stuck behind a herd of cows on the way there, having my going-away clothes and honeymoon luggage locked in a cupboard by a cleaner who'd gone home to bed, tales of arguments with a farmer and forced locks. But there were two defining moments which belonged, not in a Britcom, but as highpoints in my semi-detached religious life. The first was seeing my fiancée enter the church door, backlit by the hottest May day on record, and the second was the actual exchange of vows. At my christening, I didn't know what was happening. At my confirmation, I didn't know what I was saying. In this ancient English church filled with flowers, I made my marriage vows and felt them written through my whole being, a series of promises that would stick, made before a gathering of witnesses, and, if you believe in this kind of thing, before God, with an extraordinary light radiating across us through the west window.

On the way to the airport the next afternoon, we passed the still enigmatic Stonehenge, crawling with tourists on a May bank holiday, all none the wiser, and began our honeymoon in Madrid, which wakes up for the evening just as the average English couple are closing their eyes for the night. A little tired, we drove south through Toledo, where not much evidence remains of the most northern outpost of the Muslim emirates. Ironically, the integrated Muslim engineers and architects had been busy designing many of the finest churches in Toledo, such as the church of Santiago del Arrabal, and erecting the old city gates. These are the scenes which provide the backdrop to the renowned paintings of the Spanish ruling classes by Toledo's own El Greco.

It was only when we came to Cordoba in Andalusia that I could bear witness to the material attainments of Medieval Islam. Opposite our hotel window was the Mezquita, which means Great Mosque in Spanish, and was for centuries the most sacred place of pilgrimage in the world after the Kaaba in Mecca and the Al-Aqsa mosque in Jerusalem. It once possessed an original script of the Koran and a bone from the arm of Mohammed, neither of which are in evidence now.

To me it spoke of two things at once. Built a century before the Norman Conquests, it had been quite an open space originally, where all focus would have been directed at the main prayer niche, the mihrab, whence the words of the imam or preacher would have amplified around the building. The interior would have seemed wide and free, with a number of high, ornately decorated red and white arches, like curved candy cane. That was the Mesquita's heart.

Yet it had absorbed change too. The open space was broken by a forest of pillars added later to support another dome, and the curious effect of this was to make the building seem cloistered, like a medieval cathedral. Heightening this impression was the sixteenth-century Christian chapel with a high altar, sanctioned by Carlos V, built right in the middle. It seems sacrilegious, of course, but then it is merely the negative image of Santa Sophia in Istanbul, which was upgraded from Christianity to Islam, a complete swap in identity.

Buildings like this are greater than the sum of their parts. Cordoba is famous for its stunning patios, which are not ten square metres of decking with a garden gnome but cool court-yards celebrated every May with a Festival of the Patios. Posing deliciously on the Patio de los Naranjos, the entrance to the Mezquita where ablutions were made, was a long-legged Spanish model in a short black dress on a photo shoot for a magazine; a little Spaniard with a pot-belly was throwing the sun up at her with his silver reflector disc. Parading down the outside of the building were some hot extras in minaret hats being filmed for a movie which I was unable ever to locate – *Who Will Be King of Granada*?

Places such as this today are like Venice: their former function as a trading or religious centre has vanished, and their prospects now rely on being good to look at. If that's how they are to survive that seems fine for now, so long as we remember to pay respect to the civilisations which built them. This part of my Europe was there for us to see on honeymoon because many centuries earlier Mohammed the camel-driver had taken to retreating to the mountains outside Mecca for a serious think. That much any of us could do. But the Prophet prayed, and encountered Gabriel, and received the word of God, and spread that word faster than any religion in history. Here was one inspired, attractive and unexpected outcome in the land of tapas and San Miguel.

There is so much of Islam which most in the West have never understood, yet this religion has fostered intellectual debate, drawing on the same works of Aristotle which, with Plato and

Socrates, make a bedrock for much philosophy in the Christian world too. This can seem abstract until you imagine a judge called Ibn Rushd sitting on his patio in twelfth-century Cordoba, reading *The Incoherence of the Philosophers*, the latest work by al-Ghazali in which the influence on Islam of Aristotle *et al.* is criticised. With subjects such as the First Being, Heaven and the nature of the soul in question, Ibn Rushd was moved to write a retort from Cordoba which is regarded as the climax of Arabian thought, under the genuinely best-selling title *The Incoherence of the Incoherence*. Salman Rushdie would have been welcome on Ibn Rushd's patio, for a great vein of Islam is to do with debate and dispute over what it means; whether the words of Mohammed have been rightly interpreted by sharia, the sacred law which developed in his wake.

The two men could have discussd the Hadith, the secondary source of revelation to that which is in the Koran. The Hadith are certified stories about the life of the Prophet and therefore the basis for rules and hints about conduct. For a hundred years, modernising Muslim scholars have argued that the carefully and swiftly recorded Koran and these later additions by others should not be given equal weight. From this unhappy issue come the arguments over the equality of women, for example, which is not at issue in the Koran, but under certain parts of Hadith, gives them parity with a horse. The most shameful aspect of Rushdie's persecution after the publication of *The Satanic Verses* was the cheap shots from British columnists who wrote that he was asking for it, that he must have known Muslims could not stand criticism. This canard remains a horrible misrepresentation of Islam. At its best it is as healthily disputatious as Judaism.

Leaving Cordoba still feeling Moorish, we travelled west to Granada, wondering, like most British people, what it was about key cities from the Islamic world that they were thought suitable brand names for motorway service stations or, in the case of Mecca, a chain of bingo halls, ballrooms and trading home for the Miss World contest.

Granada's greatest pride is the palace-fortress of the Alhambra on a rocky outcrop above the city. It is where the art of the Spanish Moors reached its supreme achievement. Yet again, it is the Word which is the most critical idea in religious life. The Koran prohibits the depiction of Allah in any form, or indeed any person or animal, so Islamic artists had to concentrate on designing geometric patterns, in which the art of calligraphy is the most important form. They developed this art of writing and wrote the same phrase thousands of times across the Alhambra, repeated ad infinitum: *Wa-la ghaliba illa-Llah*. There is no Conqueror but God. In this light space it becomes more than a statement of perceived truth; it is the first abstract art.

Outside in the Generallife, the 'garden of the architect', are more evocative patios with sculpted junipers and pools of water, and a staircase where the snowmelt from the Sierra Nevada washes down the stone balustrades. To be blunt, it makes the four-square Hever Castle built two centuries later for the doomed Anne Boleyn, (which we haunted in my childhood), and its boring rectangular lake seem like a suburban semi.

The greatest of all travel writers, Jan Morris, wrote about the Alhambra: 'Life itself, which was seen elsewhere in Europe as a kind of probationary preparation for death, was interpreted by the Moors as something glorious in itself, to be ennobled by learning and enlivened by every kind of pleasure.' The right place for a honeymoon, then.

Travel to new places will change the way you think. Moorish Spain did that to me. But the course of your life can change the way you perceive these places too. Our early marriage was led very close to the Meridian line of zero longitude running south from Greenwich, and three days after our first child was born I sat on a bench watching my wife play tennis with my oldest friend, Matthew, by the rose garden where once I'd been marched up and down, being yelled at by a lapsed Catholic. It was as if all the chronometers in the Observatory had been set right again by an invisible hand.

The man-made Meridian line runs south from Greenwich through Lewes on the Sussex coast. It was the kind of place I loathed as a child when on a day trip with my parents. As a young south London parent myself, I now understood why we'd been there. Days out to the north, east and west of London involved a formidable crossing of the metropolis. Kent and Sussex were the only realistic options. Holding what proved to be an erroneous belief that driving a Ford Capri in the nineties was somehow retro-chic, I nearly slipped a disc strapping two little boys into car seats in the unreachable back seats of this red coupé and headed down the A21.

Having once found Lewes tedious beyond endurance, now I felt amazement that it had been where Henry James holed up to finish his novels. This was a rich connection for me, because he had been visited there by his fond oldest brother, William. William James had been a non-subject by the time I went to university; extra-ordinarily, since he can claim to be one of the first and greatest psychologists.

The James boys' father was a one-legged follower of the Swedenborg persuasion, a faith he had found a consolation when the family lodged in Windsor Great Park and he became obsessed with the belief that he had been in a room with a 'beast'. This 'vastation' carried him into a two-year depression, which he was helped out of by the nineteenth-century movement named after Emanuel Swedenborg, a scientific genius responsible for many advances in modern mining and the understanding of thermal physics, who after thirty years, had retired to devote the rest of his life to religion. William Blake was a follower for a while; both men saw spirits and angels from another world. Fortunately, Sweden-borg harnessed these visions to develop a benevolent theology.

God's essence is love, he said. His action is wisdom. Before the Fall, man and God were in harmony. After the Fall, man was separated from God, who pitied him, gave him the laws through Moses, and brought man upwards so that in time he appeared to man as himself man, Christ.

In short, God is Love. The Second Coming is not a physical event but the time when we attain true spiritual knowledge and pass into the world of spiritual visions, such as Swedenborg and Blake themselves had. No wonder the Victorians believed in fairies.

William James spent his life trying to make sense of his father's vastation and the comfort he drew as a Swedenborgian, but his bravest achievement, with fossil finders in the ascendant, was to use psychology to defend the right to believe. He rejected medical materialism, sexual neurosis and all other attempts to analyse away faith which were rising at the time and are still ascendant today.

Religion, he said, 'like love, like wrath, like hope, ambition, jealousy, like every other instinctive eagerness and impulse . . . adds to life an enchantment which is not rationally or logically deducible from anything else.'

That made sense on my wedding day, in Islamic Cordoba and Granada, in Greenwich Park and on the tow-path in Lewes. In many ways it stands as the opening statement for the defence of faith in an invisible God.

For just as Ibn Rushd and Salman Rushdie might have debated on a hot patio, so the history of Christianity has hosted a thousand perspectives over the centuries, each with validity to the people of the time. The key words to remember, in my view, are 'imagination', in the sense that religion wants to deal in the wonders of life and constantly interpret them; and 'humility', in that any system of thought which denounces another disrespectfully is a force for destruction.

William James resisted the idea that the new evolutionists had all the answers. Who will step forward to do this today? And what will become of the relationship between the faiths in Britain if the reward for arguing in favour of tolerance of all creeds is abuse from a powerful section of academics whose day job is science?

A Big Tent

In introducing this book, I pledged not to dodge the question: Is there Anybody up there?

Yes, I think there is.

What? How do I know?

Because of how much there is going on out there down here.

Just as we point a radio telescope to the far reaches of the universe and observe that there is H_2O in the formation of a new star system, so anyone pointing that telescope back at us would have to conclude we are religious by nature, like it or not.

A human life is spent willing into existence, out of the clear blue sky, what we desire or need. We need the next meal, and, having secured it, we progress. Our ambitions do too. We try to conjure up something interesting to do, find love, have children, try to make a good life, hope for a good death. We'd like to leave behind a good reputation if we can. Many, perhaps most, of us are bent out of shape by this process, but each of these aims begins as an intangible desire which, when attained, leaves us wanting more.

At every point in this progression through life we could choose to go it alone and calculate the odds scientifically before moving our pieces around the chessboard of life. Or we can do what nearly everyone does. Try hard and hope for the best, taking occasional inspiration and consolation on a tough journey through a god or gods or a sense of a soul or a spirit. What the atheist cannot accept, and perhaps doesn't have the empathy or imagination to see, is that on this daily journey through space and time, most people throughout the ages have found it makes more sense to have an idea of divinity than not.

In very recent times, we have answers from science to explain what once seemed inexplicable. An epileptic is not possessed by Satan. A miscarriage is not a divine punishment. Thunder is not the voice of God. The atheist is able to point to these fallacious beliefs and argue that if they have been disproved, then the rest of the territory in which gods hold sway is without truth too. This makes rational sense, but the atheist needs to look again. There are tough questions he can't dodge.

Was mankind insane to invent religion? Is all human history, therefore, an adjunct to some mass psychosis? And, if it's as clear now as it has ever been – and has been accepted by many for thousands of years – that a literal, bearded God did not make the world from divine clay, then why doesn't the desire for a spiritual life simply vanish?

My answer sounds embarrassingly like a Captain Kirk speech from *Star Trek*. If, to the atheist, the main purpose of human fertility is reproduction driven by chemical hormones in a flux of brain and body chemistry, then what is the idea of love between two souls, minds and bodies but an illusion, like religion? I fear that all the many attempts to explain love in the context of animal behaviour, the societal self-interest of altruism, and the necessary propagation of the species, make as much sense as taking a Mozart manuscript and cleverly pointing out where the staccato, pizzicato and fortissimo symbols are written. That accounts for the technical ups and downs, but says nothing about the music the composer heard in his mind's ear as he dashed out the notes on sheaves of lined paper.

Similarly with man's spiritual desires. Call him deluded, or easily manipulated, or just wrong, but he has invented these amazing stories for a reason and left behind on the surface of our planet a clear and present evidence of his desire for gods or God as real as his desire to be loved.

If there is nobody up there sitting on a cloud, we've still invented them as deliberately as we've invented the steam engine. They will not be uninvented. Let's appreciate and analyse this phenomenon by all means, but the option to ignore it is nothing but an intellectual disengagement on grounds of personal distaste.

So where's the beef? The most unpredictable and, to people of my way of thinking, infuriating evidence that the universality of the life of the soul and the spirit was persistently distinct from the deterministic science of the mind came with the phenomenon of the 'New Age' at the end of the twentieth century. This was something a devout sceptic like me should still be railing at now, but my difficulty was that it was as irresistible as a one-year-old with a radiant smile. I can call it mumbo-jumbo, Professor Dawkins can call it dangerous nonsense, but in my experience a daft idea is better dealt with by respectful laughter than by tub-thumping demands to close everything down.

It's difficult to pinpoint the dawn of this New Age because it began for different people at different times. Of course there were already some balding relics of the Age of Aquarius around, and good luck to them if they're still in it. I identify the beginning of mine to reading a barking mad, glorious, Celtic, Pagan, Christian novel called *A Glastonbury Romance* by John Cowper Powys.

Writing in 1933, the author was raised as the son of the vicar of Montacute, in sight of Glastonbury Tor. He was one of the least edited writers in the English language, giving us in over a thousand pages what could have been told in two hundred. But no novel was ever so drenched in the atmosphere of that strange Somerset landscape, lifted from out of the sea by the King's Sedgemoor Drain, which runs from deep inland via the River Perrett into the Bristol Channel.

Cowper Powys wrote an epic tale of the holy grail, but also a depiction of capitalism and communism in the thirties which climaxed in a temporary but fatal flood. The Quantock Hills, Wookey Hole, Shepton Mallett, Wells, the First Being, the Evil One, Ancient Druids and confused vicars are depicted at length until on the final page the author gives us his credo: 'The powers of reason may number the stones of Stonehenge and guess at the origin of the Grail at Glastonbury, but they cannot explain the mystery of the one, nor ask the required question of the other.'

I read *A Glastonbury Romance* in 1980, but there was a date looming later in that decade which came and went without the world ending, its significance now forgotten. The year we'd learned to dread, since our childhoods, had been 1984, when, by Orwell's prediction, we would be living in a totalitarian state. Many bad events did occur in 1984. York Minster burned down, the HTLV-III virus was identified as the cause of AIDS, Mrs Gandhi was killed after the storming of the Golden Temple, Ronald Reagan was re-elected. And a phenomenon called 'the greenhouse effect' was identified at the University of East Anglia as a likely precursor to something called 'global warming'. It was a pretty bad year for me too.

However, that which does not kill us makes us strong, and so we approached 1985 with a new mindset and a new date to fear: 'the year 2000'. We had a decade and a half left until every millennial prediction of doom would come true. So, in 1985, many minds were newly receptive to Troy Kennedy Martin's definitive nuclear conspiracy thriller *Edge of Darkness*, one of the BBC's finest dramas, in which a man is spoken to by his dead daughter and most of us were introduced for the first time to James Lovelock's concept of *Gaia*, the theory that Earth was herself an organism which would self-heal long after we had blown ourselves up. As an idea it had a unique quality; it was reassuringly fatalistic.

That year too saw John Boorman's film *The Emerald Forest*, accompanied by one of the best diaries of a film-maker at work, *Money into Light*. Shot in adverse circumstances in Brazil, it was the story of an American boy lost and brought up in the Amazon rainforest. It depicted animism in action, tribespeople sniffing a hallucinogen and believing they were an eagle flying high above the jungle, seeing what the eagle saw and feeling as it felt. I saw it in a draughty cinema and came out with a cricked neck. At a corner shop in Finsbury Park the elderly cashier saw this and said she had healing hands. Insisting that I turn around she then lay her hands on my aching shoulder and pressed. She felt she was transmitting some eternal life force from the centre of the universe as performed by healers throughout the ages. I felt she was giving me a shoulder rub. Certainly it tingled, and the entirely bene-volent effect of her hocus-pocus benefited us both.

You may be familiar with the rest. Joss sticks, jugglers at the Glastonbury Festival, yurts, healing pyramids, aromatherapy, ley lines, regression to previous lives, Sting reading Arthur Koestler and Carl Gustav Jung and trading in his *De-doo-doo-doo* for *Spirits in the Material World*.

I came closest to all this when a friend started using divining rods, not to find water but to tell the future. I didn't know she had taken this practice up, so when she asked me one afternoon to say yes to one rod and no to the other, I was slightly surprised and very embarrassed. She was apparently charging the rods with my polarity or something.

When she then asked the rods a question – 'Should Paul and his family move to Devon?' – the rods apparently said no. That helped me make a difficult decision, and we moved to Devon at the earliest opportunity. She was a Catholic too, and yet why shouldn't she think she's connected with universal oneness through two sections of a coat hanger if she wants?

The more one group objects to this, the funnier it is. None was more pompous in his objections than Dr Jonathan Miller, as the New Age dawned in the late eighties, listening on *After Dark*, a late night TV show, to a woman describing her iridology practice. The doctor was twisted up like an octopus who'd lost his way to the beach, legs and arms wrapped round the back of his head in intellectual agony. 'Oh Nineveh, Nineveh,' he wailed; but he didn't see the role his own intellectual class had played in getting to this moment. The rationalists and the scientists had told the masses that God did not exist. Their strongest arguments were on grounds of logic. They had not expected that the masses would try to meet them halfway – with pseudo-science tinged with New

Age belief. You asked for it, Doc. React how you like, but you can't just tell the patient to go away, justifying your disdain by saying that you are simply cleverer than them.

The dichotomy we are living with in Britain is that millions of us with religious empathy have become too scared to join in. If we pass a Christian *Songs of Praise* being recorded on a Cornwall seafront, we cross the road and, from a safe distance, snipe at the happiness on the faces of those taking part. Of course it can be an alienating spectacle – all the traditional hymns off the running order, new 'prayer songs' the order of the day, deploying words like 'majesty', 'king' and 'Lord' with the poetic sensitivity of a party politician. Yet if we see a similar spectacle on the banks of an Indian river with everyone dressed up in robes, we take photographs and say 'Wow'.

One group has made brave sense out of the confusion, the Hare Krishna movement which arrived in Britain in 1968. Dancing up Oxford Street with their shaved heads and tambourines, they were one of the spectacles of my childhood. What they have achieved most for young people disenchanted by Western materialism is to allow them to find a spiritual life. What would you do? Spend three years at university in grey Britain studying physics or join a group and go to an ashram, where an entire commune is ecstatically devoted to Krishna, seeking to attain permanent consciousness for the soul and salvation from the Hindu wheel of death and rebirth, finally returning to the Godhead?

Our best friend's brother, Colin, joined Hare Krishna soon after gaining a degree, and his lovely parents were very upset. Of course, what hurt most was the idea of losing him, not to a religion, but to another part of the world. They used to fly out to Delhi to see him, and they had to admit that the work his ashram was doing for villages in using advanced engineering techniques to irrigate dead soil, masterminded by Colin, was wonderful. Then a miracle happened. With the Internet came worldwide communication, and now Colin and his dad talk on videophone twice a week.

Colin's life is one of the most extraordinary I have ever known. For years he was in robes, then he was appointed CEO of Hare Krishna's worldwide business, making health bars, flapjacks and cakes. There are a lot of other vegetarians out there. For two years he swapped his robes for a suit and lived in America, using a BlackBerry and analysing balance sheets like Donald Trump. Then the job passed to someone else, and now he is back in Delhi practising Bhakti Yoga in the ashram.

The last time he was in England he shared some of the sweets made at the ashram, which he'd kept in a thin plastic bag in a pocket in his robes. He'd changed planes three times and had not had the benefit of a shower, and all the while these milky balls of sweetness had nestled next to his groin. This was the only sweet I have ever been unable to swallow, the only time I have literally palmed food into a flowerpot. We can both get this right in another life.

I suppose it is true to admit that I like religions. Showing an interest in the beliefs of others when travelling is an enlightened way into the consciousness of a people. The problem with this is that you must be prepared to be scared witless. India is the most exhilarating case in point.

The very bad news came when I was encouraged to visit an ancient shrine favoured by William Dalrymple as a spot which proved that all religions could get along, and that indeed they had for centuries. I was taken into a part of Old Delhi so decayed that I feared catching a disease with every breath. We entered a place which Hindu, Muslim (of various brands), Christians and some group I'd never heard of all considered holy. Worshippers of every faith mixed and showed mutual respect. This was said to be good.

My gut reaction was simple. Bring in a fleet of ambulances, help the poor people shuffling about on stumps, and close the place down. To a man fresh in from London it was as hellish a place as I had ever seen. It took me years of thinking about this before I could really appreciate how that course of action might have saved a few lives in the short term but would have arrogantly denied thousands of people the one shrine they could go to where they were accepted by everybody without criticism, where their humanity came before, yet was also expressed through, their various religious identities.

What it really proved to me was that perhaps you had to fall all the way down the social scale, into and beyond leprosy, to put into daily practice the tolerance which Western liberals such as me long for. That is a terrifying prospect. For the present, we are free to attempt tolerance without this terrible fall into the pit. We should use this freedom wisely.

A happier encounter came a week later when Mr Tenzin Gyatso took my hands, smiled into my face, and with that smile opened me up like a flower so that if he'd cared to he could have told me who and what I am and summarised my very essence. I was directing a camera crew pointing in his direction at the time, so this didn't actually happen, but it could have done. I consider myself allergic to false messiahs, and he wouldn't claim to be one, but he knew to the bottom of his red and yellow robes that he was a Holy Man.

Since 1959, when the Chinese finally made his presence in Tibet untenable, the Dalai Lama has been like a latter-day Buddha, travelling the world, gathering and giving knowledge. The Tibetan mantra has gone with him and become as famous as the Hare Krishna chant. *Om mani padme hum*. Hail to the jewel in the lotus. To get to the bottom of that you'll need night classes in Buddhism. Try saying it aloud. It makes you feel like a bagpipe.

My Gyatso's country, sealed off at 14,000 feet behind the world's highest mountains, came to Buddhism one thousand years after other parts of Asia. From the year of Charles I's execution, until Castro took over in Cuba, the Dalai Lamas ruled Tibet as theocrats. 'Dalai' in Tibetan means ocean, implying a vast reservoir of wisdom. 'Lama' is Tibetan for guru. The fourteenth Dalai Lama I encountered deserved his title as well as the prefix, His Holiness.

He lives in the Indian hill station of Dharamshala now, but I met him in Bangalore, where his Gelug strand of Buddhism, the 'Virtuous' school, is not satisfied merely to meditate. It engages with charitable work too, particularly the manufacture of artificial limbs. My filming with him happened by chance. I had been making a documentary on Indian cinema, and although it was wonderfully colourful, the actors and actresses I had to interview were the vainest, shallowest wannabes I had ever encountered. The Dalai Lama happened to be in town, so off we went. I hoped he would be real.

My body language coaching as a youngster was confined to looking people straight in the eye, keeping my shoulders back, and not standing with hands in my pockets. The Dalai Lama's body appeared to have been trained by a prima ballerina and a hypnotist. There is a difference between a man with a camera and a man whose job is to meditate, and I felt it that day. His smile was wider than his face, his head radiated hidden laughter and serenity. His body was open to the room.

He'd been selected by a process of identifying the reincarnation of his dead predecessor. I'd have voted for him.

'My religion is kindness,' he said.

So is mine.

By the time the eve of the year 2000 came round, we had finally succumbed to instruction from the mass media. The apocalyptic religious nutters had done what cults always do when they see a foretold date approaching with no prospect of the end being nigh: they had slipped off our radar altogether and started working on another date.

Back in the materialist realm, the media predicted the failure of every computer on the planet and acts of nuclear terrorism in Times Square and under the Eiffel Tower. We woke up the next morning and nothing had happened, except that in Britain we'd completely blown the party. I know. I was there. My wife and I were in the famous queue at Stratford underground station at

11 p.m. on 31 December 1999 surrounded by the editors of every national newspaper, the director-general of the BBC, and all the opinion formers in the country. It was the night the New Labour bullshit machine smashed into the buffers.

I won't moan, though. At least we were out, and it was free. At about 11.30 we finally arrived at the Dome, where nothing was going with a swing and we couldn't see it anyway from our seat a hundred yards from the stage. At 12.15 a.m. in the new millennium, my wife said, 'Shall we go?'; and, fearful that if we didn't we'd be trapped there until dawn, we jogged away. We ended up at a party in Brockley.

At 11.50 p.m. on 31 December 1999, a woman in a long white dress had come on to the stage with two children and said something. Nobody stopped talking, and she wasn't properly miked anyway.

The next morning I watched 'highlights' from the previous night. The woman was, in fact, the Archbishop of Canterbury, and with the two sweet children he had been delivering a specially composed Millennium Prayer.

Still, the world hadn't ended, and the computers hadn't crashed. I did wonder, however, if the Dalai Lama's people would have let him waste this once-in-a-thousand-year opportunity to broadcast the message of truth and love to the whole planet. That's if the Chinese government hadn't jammed his transmission, of course. Our man from Canterbury had failed the intenational charisma test, yet in so doing he had somehow stayed true to the hopeless, feeble and wonderful nature of his nation's Church, which in its modest claims and benevolence seemed to me the best religious bet for another thousand years.

Rory Story

There are advantages and disadvantages to being adopted as a baby. The disadvantage is obvious – you are raised by those who are not your 'natural' parents. But there is an advantage too; at least there is in my experience. Because you wake each morning not entirely sure where you came from, your natural inclination is towards keeping an open mind, to be wary of those who create closed strata in society determined by family background, wealth, education or faith. Part of me would love to wake, yawn and swing my legs out of bed knowing that I was the twelfth Earl of Whatnot, but from as far back as I can recall I actually felt like a computer which reboots every morning. All my software operated fine, but each day always seemed unwritten, my particular operating system programmed towards sharing new ideas and not reinforcing tried old certainties. I called it devout scepticism earlier.

It was not until after two of my four children were born that I discovered there was a couple in Ireland who had conceived me in London in 1961 out of wedlock, given me up for adoption, moved home to Dublin, married, and then had four more children. Of their entire enormous family, only these two people knew this had happened to them. It was a potent secret to have kept all those years, with two birth certificates extant, one for Paul and the original in the name of Rory.

My Irish family is Catholic, and indeed it is well-established now that the adoption agencies of the British mainland were substantially supplied in the decades after the war by babies from the same background. I bear no grudge against anyone in this slice of our social history, but it is worth reminding many interest groups, from priests and doctors to legislators and even feminists, that this was not dealt with very bravely at the time by any of them. More significantly, it should teach us not to throw the first stone against what we describe as 'fundamentalist' religious practices in other countries. Our own religious and government establishment was taking babies from natural parents for the prevention of shame well into the 1970s. Just as the Catholic faith should not be condemned in isolation for the problems of convents and nunneries when Anglicans were up to the same mischief; so with adoption. Many Protestant babies were given up in the same mistaken cause.

I couldn't have been more pleased, though, about pulling the Irish card out of the hat. I wasn't one of those adopted persons who wondered idly if they were related to the Royal Family, but when I did think about it I hoped vaguely that I might prove to be either Jewish or Irish. I think this was because they both seemed to have distinct cultures involving regular, social observances and festivals across the year. Woody's well-marshalled family calendar left a good impression, while the Ireland described by James Joyce in *Dubliners* seemed like the suburban Celtic cousin of Bromley. Indeed, so comfortably did my rediscovered Irish ID seem to fit that those I've met in the last ten years often think of me as entirely Irish, even though I feel English to the last atom.

There are so many implications in what happened to me that eventually they filled a book, but most relevant here is that I encountered Catholic Ireland properly and in depth at the precise moment when it was changing faster than any other country in the world. The priests whose authority made my adoption inevitable, purveyors of guilt and shame, lost almost all their power in a few short years when tales of their own illegitimate children or their paedophilia, of the evil Magdalene Laundries and their brutal corporal punishment regimes in schools, were at last spoken of and reported nationally. The response of many Irish men and women was to tell the clerical establishment, in the spirit of Jack in *Father Ted*, to feck off.

At least, that's what seems to have happened, but I am not so sure. Many in Ireland worry now that their own god-shaped hole is being filled with consumer pleasure and escalating property prices, and this may be true. The more interesting issue will come beyond the short-term, and one of the greatest religious questions of our time is whether the Church in Ireland will adapt fast enough to catch its former flock when material things are not enough.

For now, Ireland is enjoying its freedom, and there is yoga and life coaching and going to the gym, but the undercurrents of its former religion are only in temporary abeyance. It would be a tragic mistake for Rome to encourage a comeback with more of the same, to attempt to reassert its power, when in Ireland a brilliant, educated, literate and always interested population is just waiting for someone to get Christianity right second time round. In one of the supreme ironies of modern times, it could be that the seeds for the renaissance of Ireland's faith will be planted by Catholics from Eastern Europe who are flocking there through open borders to general unease.

If you are adopted, you have specialised throughout life in getting along with and loving a family which is not naturally your own, whilst also maintaining the general illusion of normality. There are much greater burdens than this in life, so I make no complaint, but it has led someone congenitally attracted to vividness and spectacle in life to be fully committed to the reality that most interaction between peoples of different tribes, classes, or faiths has to be played out in the grey light of compromise. I like the idea of a legion of United Nations peacekeepers called the People's Illegitimates, in which I would gladly serve. One could only wear the uniform if one was either adopted or prepared to swear to the adoptee view of the world that one must at all times and in all places be both flexible and mindful of the beliefs of others.

Of course it would be a nightmare posting. Off to Nigeria to patrol the border between the Muslim north and Christian south.

To India, to intervene between the rising Hindu nationalist element and the once again vulnerable Muslim minority. To Sri Lanka to persuade the Buddhist monks to butt out of national politics, and across to South Korea, where Kentucky Fried evangelism has made it one of the world's most Christian countries. It needs to be very careful rolling out the same marketing strategy through subversion in China for fear of the next World War. And so on and on, never a dull moment for the P.I.

Back up to the Golan Heights to make sure that, if they were given back by Israel, the Syrians wouldn't rain missiles on the Sea of Galilee, and down the hill to Jerusalem to remind Israel that when David Ben-Gurion founded their country it was intended to be secular. Then on to the Internet to post every comedy routine going about the '9/11' killers of New York, to show through humour that men such as this are trapped in an adolescent psychosis, not, to use a hackneyed phrase, heroes, but zeros.

Or, perhaps most difficult of all, up to Oxford on the train to stand up to Professor Dawkins, defending the right of Roger the Christian's friends to speak in tongues to our last breath. And to Roger to say that if the professor wants to form a global federation of atheists, then he has every right to say so, but that we'd have a quiet word and ask if he might refrain from being so bloody rude about everyone else.

Then we'd go to America.

Our planet seems to be approaching an awkward historical milestone. We're running out of stuff, particularly oil. Without this we'll be unable to power our cars and planes or make plastics and many textiles. We'll lose the capacity to export and import. To many this points only one way. Man will need to look to his local economy and environment again for all these things. The horse and cart will need to be reintroduced, which will be a humbling process, so it might be worth laying some ground rules for humility. No need to lose our humanity, but everything will have to get simpler. By sucking the Arctic oil dry there's only another century left of the way we live now, but unless scientists have plans for some very big solar- or nuclear-charged batteries on aeroplanes, the world is going to shrink again.

It's very hard not to think like this when you're eating a packet of Oreos at the top of a dirt track in Pennsylvanian farmland watching an Amish family trot past in a black coach pulled by a black horse. Not that you're sure they're all in there. Their seats are set so far back in the unlit cab that all you can see is a few shapes in black clothing. They don't want to be seen. Their disaster has already happened, and they've been protecting themselves against the world in these parts for nearly four hundred years. If we can understand their desire to hide away, and what is to blame for it, we can make sense of many of the religious groups in America and of the way Americans think about the world.

Lancaster County looks like a utopia now, but the rolling landscape of high white barns and picture postcard cows has been hard won by the Amish, a section of the American Mennonite community which originated from an Anabaptist wing of Christianity under the leadership of Menno Simons, a Dutch priest.

In the sixteenth century, everyone hated the Anabaptists. While both Protestant and Catholic mainstreams found some eventual accommodation with the Reformation, the Anabaptists wouldn't compromise with anyone. They held that the Bible had given them two inalienable rights and duties. First, they condemned the idea of baptising a baby when it had no idea what choice was being made for it, so sacrilegiously baptised each other. Second, they were utterly pacifist. For this they were persecuted, and like the rest of Europe's persecuted they eventually found sanctuary in America.

This is why America is so scared of Islam, of the Umma, of the notion of a jihad to make the whole world Muslim. Written in their personal histories and vividly in evidence behind the white picket fences of the Amish is that they've already fled this kind of madness once. They really don't want it in the New World. It's what so many migrant cultures have already attempted to escape from – the fleeing Pilgrim Fathers, the Irish Catholics, the Jews, the Poles, the Germans, and now the Sikhs, and even those whose brand of Islam is not in favour in the countries of their birth. America invented a new religion too, Mormonism, and persecuted that for a while, before allowing it sanctuary in Salt Lake City.

In this historical context, Professor Richard Dawkins risks being as much a force for polarisation as a jihadi. He deliberately set out to discover the most hardcore, right-wing, creationist branch of American Christianity and yelled at it in prose. Good for him. It's as if a vicar has had a dispute with medical science and then dug out some old Nazis to shout at who'd committed evil experiments in Auschwitz. They are both lunatic extremes, but it is a major empirical and philosophical error to extrapolate from encounters with either group conclusions about the greater whole.

If you spend time in America, you just have to roll with it. It's the best place in the world to drive hour after hour, flicking from a Country and Western station making you weep with loneliness to a PBS discussion on world affairs so lofty and well-informed that Radio Four seems like banter between Ant and Dec. Then on down the dial to the many types of religious broadcasting. Some of these are fabulously mad, where listeners phone in citing a biblical verse, and saying they believe it predicts the defiance of Hans Blix by North Korea's Kim Jong-il. Other stations offer kind counsel to lost teenagers. They both want your cash; but then they've got to live.

Of course there is much to dislike. Great big glass palaces broadcasting daily services preached by reverends with teeth paid for by the flock. Christianity too cosy with the bottom line. My platoon of People's Illegitimates would certainly intervene in what adoptees have the right to know about the circumstances of their birth. At present only Alaska, Oregon, Kansas, Alabama, New Hampshire and Maine allow them to see their original birth certificates, and it is to no credit of the Christian right that they are the ones playing dirty in state senates keeping these records sealed. I might let off one of my special 'Judge Not That Ye Be Judged' firecrackers there.

But there is so much to love. A prayer breakfast in Harlem, Gospel and Grits. The mere atmosphere of St Patrick's Cathedral in New York, silent in Manhattan. If these things are not to the atheist taste, that is going to be a tough reality for them, because unlike the oil they aren't going away.

The Amish's principal settlement is called Intercourse.

Chortle, as I did. Then please consider what that word actually means according to the OED.

> **Intercourse** *n*. Social communication, dealings, between individuals; communion between man and God; communication for trade purposes etc. between different countries.

Amandola

One of the few benefits of early middle age is that you can already recognise the mistakes you have to live with. This is the grim part of losing one's youth, but the beneficial part is that you've probably become who you are meant to be. My alpha and omega is my wife and family, and that could only come after youth has gone, the trade-off being that your own children can never meet the person you once were. That's not what parents are for. Yet in some ways I have crystallised into a creature my younger self could never have foreseen. I like country walks. I'm mates with the vicar. For God's sake, I'm even a parish councillor.

I feel fortunate, however, to have a number of threads in my life which have stayed unbroken over many years now, and one of the most cherished of these is my overweight soccer team, the Cake-maker's Dozen. This was formed by school friends who never quite got over the way we were made to play rugby and longed for the freedom of the round ball game. We are now in our third decade of playing together. Badly, I should add. Very badly indeed.

It is a truism of the ageing footballer that the distance they will travel to get a game is in inverse proportion to their ability to play. When we were in our pomp twenty years ago, we moaned if we had to travel from Blackheath to Wandsworth Common. Then we began to roam the country in search of ninety minutes of opposition in a similar physical state to us. Recently, we were asked to play against a team of veterans from the hill town of Amandola in the Le Marche area of Italy. We booked ourselves on to Ryanair the same day.

During that game, two national stereotypes were happily confirmed. First, the cheating, diving Italian imploring the Virgin

Mary to intervene with clasped hands and weeping when he'd just scythed the legs from under one of his opponents. Second, the plucky English loser. Six-one it was in the end. I did get one shot away, which I felt was well saved by their keeper, who took it in the guts. Afterwards he shook my hand over a porcini roll and vino rosso and told me he was seventy-two years old.

By tradition, English football teams abroad are meant to lout about in the fashion of Henry V's troops after Agincourt. I realised we had finally matured into civilised beings when, given the option of spending an afternoon carousing in an attractive bar watching *Serie A* on TV, we voted unanimously to drive miles to see the superb religious paintings of Crevelli in the town of Monte San Martino.

As I piloted the minibus back through the hills, we twittered about chiaroscuro and triptychs like Brian Sewell leading a party of bow-tied softies from the Courtauld Institute. Alas, we didn't have time to visit the nearby city of Ascoli Piceno to see Crevelli's *Madonna and Cucumber*, but I had seen it on a previous trip and was able to confirm to my interested friends that it was really more like a gherkin.

The next afternoon we were standing in a long security queue at Ancona airport, a little surprised to be just behind the yogi of a Hindu sect. We noticed him for a number of interesting characteristics. He was smothered in women followers. He had a very expensive laptop. He had red hair and beard, and pasty white skin. He was probably christened Keith.

He sat on the plane in the furthest seat back, attended by one of his devotees, and while I waited for the loo I read both what he was tapping into his laptop and a printout of an old speech being devotedly studied by the woman next to him. A management consultancy report would have been thought a haiku compared to this drivel, spattered with ifs and buts and paths to this and that. I'd have been embarrassed to read a word of it out loud, let alone spout the whole lot to a Surrey ashram. Still, each to his own.

On my way back from the loo I was surprised to see the yogi involved in an uproarious scene. While I had been at my ablutions, he must have finished his paragraph and closed his laptop. Unfortunately for him, it had clicked shut on his long, frizzy red beard, which was now entangled in the keys and the latch of the lock. With some help from his devotees, whom I noted he did not much thank, the laptop was eventually undone and his beard freed. His face was now as red as his hair. I believe this is called *karma*.

I told this story at Stansted as we waited for our luggage, and having opened a conversation on a religious theme, my flock demanded the word from on high. It was known that the centre-forward was attempting to write about religion. I could no longer avoid telling them what I really believed. It went a little like this . . .

I eased them in gently.

It's about the journey, Grasshopper, not where you arrive.

And that would be fine if we existed on private planets, interacting only with close family and friends of identical persuasion. Awkwardly, there are six billion of us circling the sun, and a separatist answer failing to take into account the effect of one system of belief on another won't wash. Luckily, I said, I had a patented solution. It came, I thought, in three parts.

Part One. It is a given that we all have an innate predisposition to see in our surroundings the influence of the tooth fairy, Father Christmas, the little people and in time the gods, and I hoped the book I was in the middle of writing might somehow offer evidence of this through the mighty power of the anecdote. They all said, all right, we'll buy it on Amazon, so get on with it.

Well, I said, even the most sceptical soul is affected by holding their own child or seeing the sun set over the Pacific. Hollywood calls it wonder, and makes billions from it. This is because wonder really exists, and for many people that is perfectly sufficient. They are content to muddle through. But with six billion people on the case, it's unsurprising that this wonderment is expressed by others in many different ideas. End of Part One.

I had my audience. The baggage carousel was stock-still. The alternative to listening to me was to listen to the airport announcements about boarding at gate ten.

I resumed. Part Two. This could all be rather easy if it ended there, but it does not. We also have an innate tendency, beyond refutation and now hardly worth struggling with, to write the exegesis behind these different ideas. Many hope they've cracked the big one, so they discuss it with others, find common cause, meet in the same places, and give themselves a permanent brand of faith. This too is fine so long as you don't live in a part of the world where a particular form of religious observance is compulsory. But in reality, religion has been unable to resist the lure of developing and formalising these ideas, making buildings for them, founding institutions. This happens. It will happen for as long as there are men. So, point two, we have to find a way to live with this.

Still no baggage, and they were still listening.

'The third point,' I announced, 'is the key.' People like keys.

Not even Professor Dawkins can stop One and Two. There will be wonder, and it will be formally expressed. He simply has his finger in the dyke. If life was lived in a laboratory, perhaps he could stop them, though attempts by governments in the past have come to even uglier outcomes than allowing people to get on with it. However, I agree that the combination of One and Two with an evangelising zeal to convert is toxic and uncivilised.

'So, Three binds it all together.'

I could hardly wait for point three myself.

Three is a devout acceptance of the belief of others. The fundamental tenet of any faith must be to ardently support the need to understand other religions' points of view, including atheism. The great faiths and the lesser alike must recalibrate their first principles to this effect. Do not try to convert, do not judge, do not invade. Make one of those Venn diagrams and concentrate on the points where the faiths overlap in agreement. Then laud these to high heaven.

With that point we can flourish. Without it we will kill each other. There are good stories about the Apocalypse in most religions. It may prove useful to begin exploring them.

The luggage was going round the carousel now and the comments of Stansted's own Luther were thrown open to the floor. Anyone who had children knew that this process had begun. One of my daughters had just made a game called Hindopoly for school. Religious Education has changed completely. In British schools, respect and tolerance of all faiths is on the curriculum, and it has come just in the nick of time.

The average twelve-year-old now knows what a mosque, temple, church and synagogue are, and has a beginner's understanding of what goes on within. My confused generation of plump footballers at the airport will soon be able to ask their children what it's all about. All we need is the time for this to take root.

My friends have followed a similar adventure in faith and doubt to me. It's a generational thing. As I said goodbye to them at the airport, one of them smiled and spoke the old pay-off line from the Irish comedian, Dave Allen.

'Goodnight, Paul,' he said, 'and may your god go with you.'

I walked back towards him. He's just the most loveable little man you could ever meet. At my wedding he was selected to turn the music for the organist, on the basis of his grade 4 violin, but turned three pages at once and brought a solo by the star chorister to a grinding halt.

I gave him a hug.

'There's a point four,' I said. 'Can we make sure we never stop telling these stories?'

Acknowledgments

For moving in mysterious ways, I thank Delia Napier, Guy and Amelia Ashton, Jon Claydon, and Michael and Ann Brennan. For boosting morale along the way, Kate and Greg Mosse, Kate and Bill Aylward, Annette, Ata, Felix, Oscar and Leila Yoosenfinejad. For America, Diane Kavantjas, Tom, Mika and Paola Farer, Shane Brennan, Rowan Gillespie, Martin Hart, Karen Keninger and the huge Conway clan. For Italian affairs, Victoria and Matthew Gwyther, Crispin and Wilfred Aylett, David Chandler, and all the Cakemakers. For distant Alleynian matters, thanks to all back then, particularly the late Laurie Jagger, who encouraged prose and marked it generously, and Patrick Cremin for his memory banks. For supporting my writing and offering kind comments, many friends from east Devon, west Dorset and south London. For letting me score occasionally, the men of Axe Wednesday. For love, companionship on our travels, and religious debate, Tara, Sasha, Benja and Jake Arnott, and Lydia Conway. Finally, for retaining her title as the most unerring and supportive of editors, Jocasta Hamilton.